Soothing Rain

Living Water to Refresh Your Soul

Sue Summers
John 7:38

TONYA JEWEL BLESSING & SUE SUMMERS

Names: Blessing, Tonya Jewel and Summers, Sue (previously Sue Lockwood Summers)
Title: Soothing Rain: Living Water to Refresh Your Soul
Description: Littleton, Colorado : Capture Books, [2017] |
Soothing Rain: Living Water to Refresh Your Soul
| Does not include bibliographical references and index.
Identifiers: ISBN: 978-0-9978976-3-0

BISAC: EDU059000 EDUCATION / Teacher & Student Mentoring
REL006700 RELIGION / Biblical Studies / Bible Study Guides
SEL032000 SELF-HELP / Spiritual
Subjects: Women/ Bible studies /Workbook/Lessons/Workshops

Cover art: Kathryn Swezy
Interior design: Tracy Fagan
Authors: Tonya Jewel Blessing and Sue Summers
(previously Sue Lockwood Summers)
Special thanks goes to our editor, Chelsea Bezuidenhout
Contact: Capture Books www.CaptureBookstore.com
Capture Books/Twitter or Facebook, Tonya Jewel Blessing/Facebook or Sue Summers/Facebook
5856 S. Lowell Blvd. Suite 32-202
Littleton, Colorado 80123
All rights reserved.
ISBN: 978-0-9978976-3-0

Table of Contents

Forward

It has been a delight to co-author "Soothing Rain" with my dear friend, Sue Summers. I am praying that our readership will listen with their hearts to what is written, feel inspired and empowered by what is shared, and pass along the truths they learn and live to others.

I am also praying that "Soothing Rain" will be used in group studies for women. Wonderful moments are created when women come together to study God's Word, pray, share their hearts, and encourage each other in their faith walk.

The word "leadership" is used time and time again in this study. There are numerous definitions and opinions about what this term means. In order to lay a foundation for the devotional, I wanted to share my personal views on women in leadership. I believe that all women are called to lead. Some women lead in the corporate world, others in ministry arenas, in communities, local churches and, very importantly, in their families.

Leadership is not something to be taken lightly. Others are listening to what we say and observing how we live. Leading is not something we aspire toward - it simply is who we are.

May the Lord use you and those who study this material with you to impact their world.

~ Tonya Jewel Blessing

It is my ongoing desire to help children, teens, and adults become critical thinkers. The focus should always be to examine each situation and decision using God's Word as the grid of Truth. I wrote the study questions in this devotional to expand and challenge your ideas, perceptions, and their applications to your life.

~ Sue Summers

Dedication

Idella Kercher – our roots and lives will always be tangled. Thank you for being a friend and mentor to so many women.

~ Tonya Jewel Blessing

God has lovingly provided me with amazing family members and friends. This book is dedicated to each one of you who makes my life exciting and who richly blesses me every day. Thank you!

~ Sue Summers

1 Lending to God

My husband and I used to live on a rutted, dirt road east of Denver. Our home rested on the south side of the road. During spring time, the black and white cattle with their yearlings grazed on the north side. One morning late in May, a woman from the city decided to go for a ride in the peaceful, quiet country. When a semi–truck hauling grain passed her compact car on the narrow road, she panicked, over–steered, and rolled her vehicle into the grassy field across the street from our home. The heifers and calves gathered round to stare at their mutual predicament.

We decided to become more welcoming than the heifers and calves. A glass of water, a gentle embrace, and kind words provided the environment for her to share her struggles with divorce, depression, loneliness, finances, and health concerns.

The Bible says in Proverbs 19:17 (NIV) that when we show kindness to the poor we are lending to God. *"Whoever is kind to the poor lends to the Lord, and he will reward them for what they have done."* Our new friend wasn't "poor" in the physical sense, but she was certainly poor in spirit. God has a heart for those living in poverty - whether they are struggling for physical or spiritual nutrition. The Bible defines the poor as people who are weak, deprived, needy, empty, and withered. In the original text of this verse showing kindness meant bending down, or stooping over; sitting face to face with someone in need; looking them in the eyes with the love of Christ; offering friendship; uniting our lives with their lives for the purpose of easing their burden. In fact, the word "lending" means to weave together.

When we "lend" our kindness to others, the LORD becomes involved in our efforts. He aids us in our service to those in need. The Bible says that He even rewards us. He brings restoration, peace, and safety to our lives. He gives us strength to finish our spiritual race.

May the LORD continue to use us both as individuals and collectively, to lend to those in need both physically and spiritually.

week 1 reflections

1. Were you surprised that we are to LEND to God? Describe your reactions.

2. The word, "lend", means to "weave together." Explain how this fits with the content of the devotional.

3. The Bible defines the poor as *"people who are weak, deprived, needy, empty, and withered."* Reflect on some instances in your life when you aided the poor and consider your resulting feelings.

4. Reread Proverbs 19:17. What new insights did you gain?

2 Measuring the Marigolds

I like the bright yellow and orange colors of marigolds. I often plant them in pots with pansies. They always remind me of a poem by Hans Christian Anderson, *"Inchworm, inchworm, measuring the marigolds. You and your arithmetic will certainly go far. Inchworm, inchworm, measuring the marigolds. Seems to me you'd stop and see how beautiful they are."*

I don't think that life is meant to be measured in inches. Inchworms have such a limited view of their surroundings. Yet, I've found myself, at times, scrutinizing life with a ruler – examining every inch of my journey and making judgments with limited vision.

A number of years ago, a friend gave my husband a yardstick that had been printed incorrectly. The measurements weren't accurate. My measurements aren't always accurate either. Measuring life and all its complexities must be examined in light of God's Word – through His eyes, not my own.

In Ezekiel 47 (NLT), the LORD gave the Prophet Ezekiel an insightful lesson about measurements. *"Measuring as he went, he took me along the stream for 1,750 feet and then led me across. The water was up to my ankles. He measured off another 1,750 feet and led me across again. This time the water was up to my knees. After another 1,750 feet, it was up to my waist. Then he measured another 1,750 feet, and the river was too deep to walk across."*

The stream source, in Ezekiel's math instruction, was the temple of God, the place where God's presence dwelt. At first, the stream was a mere trickle, but as it flowed out it became deeper and deeper until it was too deep to walk through. When measuring life, I must start spiritually. Where am I in my walk with God? Is His presence abiding in me and working through me? Am I seeing my world through the eyes of Christ? Am I growing spiritually? Is the water rising with each measurement taken?

I don't want to be an inchworm. Besides the fact that they are green and only attractive to other inchworms – I want a bigger view of life. I want God's eternal perspective – not my limited vision.

I'm so thankful that I know women who have an eternal perspective. It's a great blessing to have found women I can walk among who look beyond limited vision into the heart of God.

week 2 reflections

1. Think about the words in the devotional: *"I don't think that life is meant to be measured in inches. Inchworms have such a limited view of their surroundings. Yet, I've found myself, at times, scrutinizing life with a ruler – examining every inch of my journey and making judgments with limited vision."* Reflect on a time when you had a "limited view of your surroundings."

2. Our heavenly Father is infinite, knowing no boundaries. We often place parameters on our thinking and our actions. What could you accomplish if you had no boundaries?

3. Consider the exact requirements God gave Noah when He commanded him to build an ark. Read Genesis 6:9-22. Why do you think God was so specific in His measurements?

4. If your life is to "measured" by obedience and faith, reflect on how yours would "measure up." Record an instance where you struggled and saw growth.

3 *What's in a Name?*

In Scripture, names have definite meanings. People and places were often named according to circumstances, characteristic traits, and physical appearance. For example, the name Rebecca means "tied up." Some Bible scholars say her beauty was so astounding that people became tongue-tied in her presence. Names on occasion were even changed. In Scripture, Jacob went from being Jacob "the deceiver" to Israel "the one who wrestled with God."

For a number of years, I worked with a team of ladies doing ministry on Pine Ridge Reservation in South Dakota. The Lakota women are unique, talented, and beautiful. I am honored to call a number of them my friends. The Lakota people have interesting names. Similar to the following list I created: Angie Respects Nothing, Laura Yellow Horse, Ruth Blacksmith, Annie Two Bulls. Their names are part of their heritage. Somewhere in Laura's lineage a relative owned a yellow horse. Ruth comes from a long line of blacksmiths. In days past, the Lakota also practiced the art of name changing. Deeds of courage, acts of kindness, and even bad behavior could result in one's name being altered.

I've enjoyed having "Blessing" as a last name. When Chris and I were engaged, the girls I worked with would gather around my desk and sing the old hymn, "Make Me a Blessing." In our culture, I wonder if names were changed based on character, behavior, or appearance, if my name would still be "Blessing." Perhaps I would now be called "Tonya Grumpy" or "Tonya Many Shoes."

What's in a name is a valid question these days. Do we reflect the name "Christian" - Christ-like or follower of Christ - in how we live? Are we a reflection of Jesus? Do we model His grace, compassion, and love? Are the fruits and gifts of the Spirit evident in our lives?

For a long time, I've had the privilege of working with a women's organization called "Women of Vision." In the original Hebrew text the definition for the word "vision" is very insightful. It means to have a dream or a revelation. It also means to prophesy. This organization is comprised of amazing women who dream big. They've been given a revelation from God to minister to the poorest in our world, and they are brave enough to prophesy, or to speak God's plan, for those who are struggling.

week 3 reflections

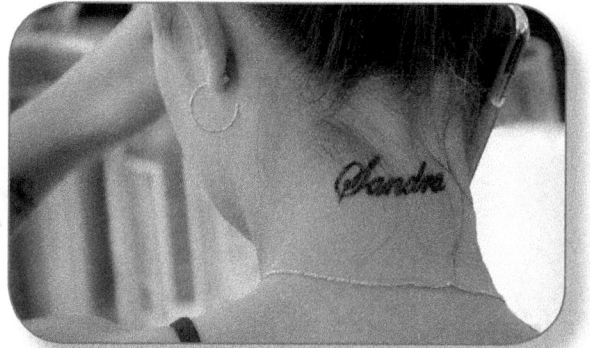

1. Consider your first name. Does it have a meaning or is it a creation of your parents? Google the meaning of your first name and reflect on the results.

2. Consider the words in the devotional, *"Deeds of courage, acts of kindness, and even bad behavior could result in one's name being altered."* What might your name be based on this tradition?

3. What considerations are typically given when naming children?

4. We all know people who consider themselves Christians, but strike us as "far from it." What specific characteristics are implied by the term, "Christian"?

4 Quiet Influence

I've been wearing the same perfume for over 30 years. Every once in a while, I briefly try something new, but so far I've always reverted back to the familiar. The scent seems to fit me. It leaves its mark, but yet isn't overpowering. It's a soft blend of earthly tones that I think compliments me. Influence is like a fragrance. It lingers. The scent is a reminder of something spoken or shared.

I'm not an "I am woman, hear me roar..." kind of gal. I prefer to live my life with grace and beauty - gently walking and touching the lives of others with more of a purr than a roar. The Bible encourages women in 1 Peter 3:4 to cultivate inner beauty, the gentle, gracious kind that God delights in. In living for Christ, I want to leave my mark, footprints that show me walking beside someone else in his or her journey. I don't want to go a single day without influencing someone for Jesus.

I pray this prayer, "I will follow You with a pure heart. Show me the people you want me to impact with biblical principles, a listening ear, and encouragement for the journey of life."

Every woman's fragrance is different - even if the perfume is the same, once mixed with an individual's body chemistry the scent changes. Some fragrances are subtle, others a little more pronounced. The same is true of the inner beauty referred to in 1 Peter 3:4. Gentleness and graciousness look different on different women.

May our fragrance linger and be a reminder of God's amazing love and grace – as a "quiet influence".

week 4 reflections

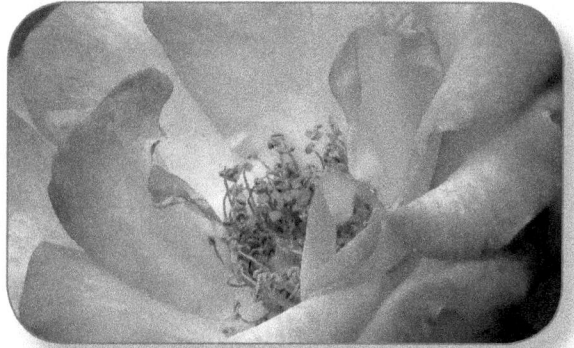

1. The devotional states, *"Influence is like a fragrance. It lingers. The scent is a reminder of something spoken or shared."* Do you agree with this thought? Why or why not?

2. Consider some people who have been "quiet influences" in your life. In what ways did they impact you?

3. Read 1 Peter 3:4 in several different versions of the Bible. (Go to biblegateway.com for an easy-to-use website for various translations.) Then write it in your own words in "today's" language.

4. List specific ways you could be a "quiet influence" on family members, friends, or neighbors.

5 Is Heaven in the Yellow Pages?

While doing some research recently on the internet, I came across this very moving poem:

> *"Mommy went to Heaven, but I need her here today. My tummy hurts and I fell down; I need her right away. Operator, can you tell me how to find her in this book? Is heaven in the yellow part? I don't know where to look. Maybe if I call her, she will hurry home to me. Is heaven very far away; is it across the sea? Help me find the number please; is it listed under 'Heaven'? I can't read these big, big words. I am only seven. I'm sorry, operator. I didn't mean to make you cry. Is your tummy hurting too, or is there something in your eye? If I call my church, maybe they will know. Mommy said when we need help, that's where we should go."*
>
> *(author unknown)*

I know some of the poem's phrases are outdated. Most people don't use the Yellow Pages these days, and, with computerized services, operators are a rare commodity. Yet the yearning of a young child for his or her mother moves my heart. All kinds of thoughts and images of the child came to mind. How long has his or her mother been gone? Who is taking care of the child? What does he or she look like? Who is reading this seven-year-old bedtime stories and rubbing noses for Eskimo kisses?

When I read the last stanza, I am brought to tears, *"If I call my church, maybe they will know. Mommy said when we need help, that's where we should go."* There are churches all over our cities that are resourceful and safe places for grieving families to go. But the church is more than a name, a building, or even the pastor. According to Scripture, believers in Jesus are the Church.

As women who know Jesus, we're the mothers to those who have no moms. We're the ones who tend to tummy aches and bandage scraped knees. We read stories and place gentle kisses on the tear-stained cheeks of the hurting. We give voice to the struggling, abused, and bruised. We dig wells, feed the malnourished, and find jobs and homes for struggling young adults. We know the secrets of heaven, and hold keys that help others who are caught in grief and uncertainty find a place of rest and peace.

Most of us have never worked as a telephone operator. But we have worked and will continue to work in sharing our time, resources, and the truths of eternity with those struggling in our communities and around the world.

week 5 reflections

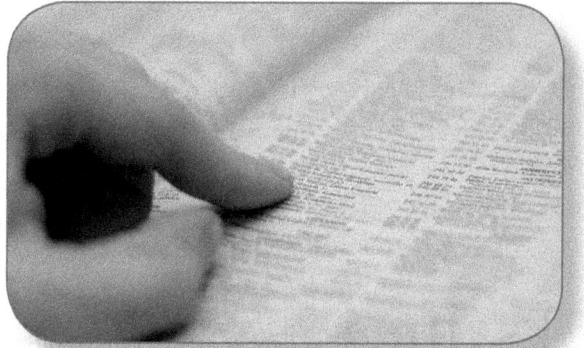

1. Reread the poem at the beginning of the devotional. What thoughts and feelings do you experience?

2. According to the poem, the child's mother has gone to heaven, and the child *needs* her. Explain the relationship a child develops with his/her mom. What unique role does a mother fill that another never can?

3. Think about your own mother. What kind of influence did she have on your life?

4. According to Scripture, the body of Christ is the church. How can adults in a church positively serve the community? In what specific ways can your church reach out to those in need?

To Be or Not to Be a Tree

6

Psalm 1 is one of my favorite passages of Scripture, *"...they find joy in obeying the Law of the LORD, and they study it day and night. They are like trees that grow beside a stream, that bear fruit at the right time, and whose leaves do not dry up. They succeed in everything they do."* Psalm 1:2-3 (GNB)

I remember memorizing these life-changing words as a young teenager. The truth and value of God's Word is timeless. Weather can change moment by moment. Yesterday, it was 70 degrees Fahrenheit and sunny; today, it is 40 and overcast. Who knows what tomorrow will bring? But the life-changing power of Psalm 1 is as real to me today, as it was all those years ago.

When we obey (listen, pay attention, and follow) the Bible, and study what it has to say, as if our next breath depended upon its truths, we grow as individuals. We are changed in our physical being, our emotional make-up, and our spiritual walk. We become like trees with deep roots that are tapped into something beyond our comprehension. Without struggling, striving, or stressing, we are refreshed and quenched from a deep thirst that we cannot understand ourselves or explain to others. We begin to bear fruit and reproduce the things of God in our lives. The fruit that we grow is pleasant and sweet, like watermelon on a hot summer day, or fresh squeezed orange juice that awakens our taste buds on a sleepy morning. Those around us enjoy what God is doing in our lives, and have the privilege of resting under our branches. We're timely in what we do and what we say. Our lives seem to be in sync. We don't wither. We don't faint or grow weary but are blessed and succeed in all that we do.

At my childhood home in Ohio, there's a tree in the backyard that my sister planted as a Girl Scout project many, many years ago. The tree has sustained life in spite of drought, blight, thunderstorms, snowstorms, and insect infestation. It hasn't withered. In fact, it has brought great pleasure to my family. We've picnicked under the tree, sharing food, song, and story. At one point, there was a tire swing tied to one of the branches. The sturdiness of the tree allowed us to sway to and fro, creating a cool breeze on a hot summer day.

May the verses of Psalm 1 ring true in our hearts today and in our seasons to come. *"Oh Lord, I live by your word. I'm like a tree by a stream. I'm bearing fruit. My leaves are green. Oh Lord, I live by your word..."* (Kent Henry – musical artist)

week 6 reflections

1. Locate and read Psalm 1 in several different Bible translations. (You can go online to biblegateway.com to easily do this.) Reflect on the thoughts you have about this Scripture.

2. As you consider the comparison to trees, what comes to mind? Do you have a "tree story" from your past? If so, summarize it here.

3. "Bearing fruit" is often referred to in Scripture. In what ways could you bear fruit?

4. Reread the third paragraph in this devotional. It's uplifting. How do these words encourage you?

7 Salt and Light ~ Part 1

Chris and I had steak for dinner recently. When I took our meal out of the oven it was sizzling in the cast iron broiler pan and looked simply delicious. When I took my first bite - it was good but something was missing. A little bit of salt was needed. The salt enhanced the flavor of not only my steak but my baked potato as well.

God has called us to be salt and light. Our main role in this world is to enhance or flavor the lives of others with the love and grace of Christ. *"Let your light thus shine before men, so that they may see your upright works, and glorify your Father who is in the heavens."* Matthew 5:16 (DBT)

We serve a BIG God. Whether in the United States or in other regions of the world, we can't be afraid to serve a God of big tastes.

In many cultures salt is not only used for flavoring but for cleansing and disinfecting. In Bible times newborn babies were rubbed with salt. Light is also a common metaphor used in Scripture: God is light, those who don't know Jesus are without light, light shouldn't be hidden under a bushel, God's light shines through His children, and Jesus, the sinless Son of God, is the ultimate light.

When I was growing up there were only two kinds of salt available at the grocery store: "iodized" and "non-iodized." These days there are numerous salt choices: Himalayan pink salt, Celtic salt, and Maldon salt, just to name a few. There are also numerous light bulb choices: incandescent, florescent, halogen, and then there's the variety of wattages. Scripture calls us to be salt and light. Different salts uniquely flavor food. Different types of light are needed for different settings.

It is important that our salt doesn't lose its flavor and that our light doesn't grow dim. If something isn't palatable people will reject it. If something isn't clearly illuminated people will become confused and walk away. Providing light and seasoning to someone's life is a spiritual calling. As women who influence others, we must be sensitive to how much, when, and in what manner salt is applied. The same can be said for light. Light comes in many different forms. Sometimes a candle is needed and sometimes a spotlight works best.

May the LORD use us to enhance, flavor, and illuminate our world.

week 7 reflections

1. Consider this Scripture: *"Let your light thus shine before men, so that they may see your upright works, and glorify your Father who is in the heavens."* Matthew 5:16 (DBT) Reflect on some "Christians" you have met who seemed to have "lost their light."

2. Why do you think the Scripture refers to "saltiness"? List some various uses of salt over the years.

3. The rest of the Scripture quoted in this devotional states: *"Neither do you light a lamp, and put it under a measuring basket, but on a stand; and it shines to all who are in the house. Even so, let your light shine before men; that they may see your good works, and glorify your Father who is in heaven."* Matthew 5:14-16 (WEB) In your own words, what do you think this means?

4. If someone you know needed clarification about being "salt and light to the world," how would you explain this metaphor in real life?

8 *Salt and Light ~ Part 2*

In ministry life, I have felt pressured, a number of times, to shrink myself. I'm not by nature a spotlight person. In private, I'm a quiet person. I don't like people staring at me. I don't like a great deal of attention. In South Africa, however, I have been pushed to the forefront, in part, because I'm American, also because of the color of my skin, and my gender. I don't look like most South Africans; I don't sound South African; without saying a word even my clothes and mannerisms set me apart. My husband has told me more than once, "Please, baby, quit waving your hands all over while you're talking. You're going to hit someone."

Jesus said, *"You are the light of the world. A city that is set on a hill cannot be hidden. Nor do they light a lamp and put it under a basket, but on a lampstand, and it gives light to all who are in the house. Let your light so shine before men, that they may see your good works and glorify your Father in heaven."* Matthew 5:14~16 (NKJV)

Remember the movie, "Honey, I Shrunk the Kids"? A father, with good intentions, accidently uses his newly invented shrinking machine on his children. In truth, there have been times when I've shrunk myself spiritually. I've worried that my faith makes others uncomfortable, or that sharing eternal truths might offend. Shrinking who I am as a Christian should be just as uncomfortable as wearing a cotton shirt that I've accidently shrunk in hot water - it just doesn't fit right. Once, when I was substitute teaching, I noticed a saying on the teacher's desk. *"Your playing small doesn't serve the world. There is nothing enlightened about shrinking so that other people won't feel insecure."* (Anonymous)

I've reached the decision that if shrinking myself means disobedience to what God has called me to do then I am actually shrinking the power and Word of the LORD in my life. I don't want my own insecurities to prevent me from serving God with the gifts and talents He's given me. I also don't want to allow someone else's insecurities to drive me to the shadows. In that same vein, I want confidence in my heart, so jealousies and insecurities don't cause me to want someone else to diminish on my behalf. Shrinking only diminishes flavor and illumination. *"You are the salt of the earth...You are the light of the world...Let your light shine before men, that they may see your good deeds and praise your Father in heaven."*

week 8 reflections

1. Are you more yourself when you're alone or with others? Share some insights about your personal comfort level.

2. Sometimes we "shrink" so that others will not feel overpowered by our knowledge, our devotion to God, or our personality. We sometimes feel intimidated by the people around us - or perhaps the situation we find ourselves in. We shrink rather than proclaim any "good news." It seems uncomfortable to speak about the truth we know to be true. Reflect on the last time you felt this "shrinkage" and share how you could have handled it in a winsome way.

3. The devotional states: *"Your playing small doesn't serve the world. There is nothing enlightened about shrinking so that other people won't feel insecure."* (Anonymous) What do you think this means?

4. There are many types of salt to buy and a variety of light bulbs to purchase. Each fits a particular purpose. How does this relate to our individual gifts as believers?

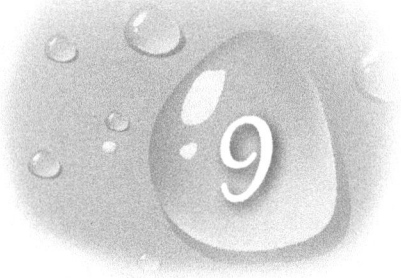

9 *My Life Song*

I recently had the privilege of filling in for our pastor. He and his family were enjoying a much-needed vacation. It's always an honor to receive an invitation to share God's Word. My message was entitled, "My Life Song." What I shared was based on Psalm 23 (NLT). This passage was written by King David, probably in his later years. The verses are truly a life song describing his personal seasons of tranquility, toil, trial, and tenderness as a shepherd boy, and later as king of a nation.

"The LORD is my shepherd; I have all that I need. He lets me rest in green meadows; he leads me beside peaceful streams," is such a vivid picture of the peace and tranquility that only the Good Shepherd can provide. David also understood the seasons of toil or work in his life song. *"He renews my strength. He guides me along right paths, bringing honor to his name."* The following verses depict a season of trial. *"Even when I walk through the darkest valley, I will not be afraid, for you are close beside me. Your rod and your staff protect and comfort me. You prepare a feast for me in the presence of my enemies. You honor me by anointing my head with oil..."* David included in his life song that whenever there's a trial, there's always a table set by God with food prepared by His own hand. The final verses in Psalm 23 (NLT) depict a season of tenderness, *"...My cup overflows with blessings. Surely your goodness and unfailing love will pursue me all the days of my life, and I will live in the house of the LORD forever."* David had experienced time and time again God pursuing him. He knew that the goodness and love of the LORD was abundant.

The message content came from some personal spiritual evaluation. I've been contemplating lately the lyrics of my life song. *"For we are his workmanship, created in Christ Jesus unto good works, which God hath before ordained that we should walk in them."* Ephesians 2:10 (KJV) What does the music of my life sound like? It is pleasant to those around me? Can my lyrics even be heard? Most importantly, does my life song reflect the good works that God ordained for me to sing?

week 9 reflections

1. Think about your favorite hymn or praise song. Take time to sing it or listen to it. Why do you think this song holds such a special place in your heart?

2. Read and then reread the 23rd Psalm. This is often shared at funerals or memorial services. What about this particular psalm gives comfort to those who are grieving?

3. Why do you think certain songs evoke significant emotional responses?

4. Consider your "life song." What elements of your song would be manifested in the lyrics which God Himself might enjoy? (For example: compassion, spirit, boldness, conviction, etc.) List some words that you'd like others to "sing" about you.

10 *Comfort*

I had an encounter a number of weeks ago with a friend that initially left me feeling disappointed. I had shared what I considered to be important personal information, and my expectations were that my friend would respond in a certain way. I wanted her reassurance, her support, and comfort; I wanted her to offer prayer on my behalf and tell me that she loved and valued me. Instead, the conversation that I'd played over in my mind ahead of time, consisted of a few heartfelt words from me, and very little verbal response from my friend.

It's never good to enter into communication with preconceived ideas of how a person will respond. Those kinds of expectations set us up for disappointment. I wanted comfort and encouragement on my terms and in my way. When I was able to look beyond my expectations, I noticed tears welling in her eyes. Those tears were her expression of comfort. She was moved by my need, and doing the best she could in that moment to give me reassurance.

Pamela McQueen has this to say about comfort, *"When we hurt, God offers us comfort. No trouble is so large or so small that He will not help. But when we have received His strength for the trouble at hand, do we share it in return? Comfort isn't meant to be hidden away, but passed on to those in similar need..."*

A gentle embrace, a heartfelt prayer, kind words, an act of service, and yes, even tears mean so much to those who are hurting. I'm so glad the LORD doesn't hide His comfort from us. This expression of love is freely given, and in return should be freely shared. How can we have a lifestyle that offers comfort? *"Who comforts us in all our tribulation, that we may be able to comfort those who are in any trouble, with the comfort with which we ourselves are comforted by God."* 2 Corinthians 1:4 (NKJV) If we are imitators of God, we should be women who are able to share comfort in many forms: a financial gift, a simple present, ministering to a child in need, reading and sharing God's Word, cooking a meal, teaching life skills, helping the poor in body and the poor in spirit.

May we continue to receive the comfort of God, and to freely share that same comfort with others.

week 10 reflections

1. Describe a time or place that you consider "comfortable." What makes it feel so comforting?

2. The devotional states: *"It's never good to enter into communication with preconceived ideas of how a person will respond. Those kinds of expectations set us up for disappointment."* Often we anticipate the responses of others (husbands perhaps???) and then are left feeling saddened by the perceived lack of compassion. Contemplate a better approach to communication that wouldn't evoke disappointment.

3. Think about a friend you have who needs comfort right now. How can you specifically comfort her?

4. God comforts us. He has promised to be with us through all of life's circumstances. How does this help you as you deal with difficulties?

11 Resources for the Journey

Quite some time ago, I helped organize a fall day retreat for women. The retreat was centered around Proverbs 31:10, *"Who can find a strong, courageous, virtuous, and resourceful woman? She is more precious than jewels."* (paraphrased) One of the sessions for the retreat was called, "Resources for the Journey." I believe that the women in my life, on a personal level and in ministry, are resourceful. Some of the synonyms for resourcefulness are: able, bright, capable, clever, creative, fertile, imaginative, ingenious, innovative, inventive, quick-witted, sharp, and talented.

My favorite synonym is "fertile." My husband built a raised vegetable garden this spring. He's starting to harvest the fruits of his hard work. When he prepared the garden, he was careful to include a water system, excellent soil, good drainage, and, of course, the needed seeds.

I believe that we need to be fertile. Seed beds need to be prepared to reach others for Jesus. The soil of ministry needs to be worked, weeded, and watered. The seeds need to be planted in our city, state, and around the world.

I'm bold enough to believe that if the garden has been planted and is being faithfully tended that God will provided the on-going resources for the ministry. I also believe that He will provide the personal resources we need. He often does the providing through continued anointing upon my resourceful friends.

I have been truly blessed to have strong, courageous, and virtuous women in my life. They are shining examples of Christ embodied. I have no doubt that each and every one of them, given the opportunity, would fight valiantly, slay dragons, and rescue others in distress. Their suit of armor would include a seasoned life of prayer, the power of God's Word, and compassion for those held captive. My only concern is that their tears of love would rust their knightly attire.

week 11 reflections

1. Reread Proverbs 31:10. Your first reaction might be: "there can't be such a woman." However, think about women who have served as role models or mentors in your life. List their attributes or characteristics.

2. "Resourceful" is not a word we often use to describe others. What does this word personally mean to you?

3. Consider your church or a favorite non-profit organization. What resources does it use to be effective? How can you be involved as a "resource" for that organization?

4. List people in your life you would consider to be *"able, bright, capable, clever, creative, fertile, imaginative, ingenious, innovative, inventive, quick-witted, sharp, and talented."* How do they enrich your life?

12 *Driven to Drive*

It's interesting who you can meet and what you can learn about people during a three-hour wait at the Colorado Driver's License Bureau. Recently I had to renew my driver's license. After obtaining my ticket number, I went next door to a consignment store. With my purchase of a new purse and shoes bagged, I exited the store, stepped over a gentleman who had fallen asleep on the sidewalk outside, and re-entered the Driver's License facility.

I immediately made a new friend there. My new gal pal had just moved from Midwest America to Colorado. She now enjoyed both her grandchildren and the weather. Eventually our conversation moved onto deeper issues – like the moral dilemma of whether it's okay to lie about your weight on your driver's license. I also observed a frustrated woman struggling with a language barrier, and a determined elderly gentleman renewing his driver's license. His license had been expired for over a year, so the law required him to take the written test. He didn't pass. When the attendant reviewed the missed answers with him, he requested to take the test a second time. He didn't pass. When the same attendant explained that you could only mark one correct answer per question, he requested to take the test a third time. He passed – and moved forward with the eye exam – which he didn't pass.

I also met a young man obtaining his driver's license for the first time, and I actually had a conversation with "Mr. Sleeping on the Sidewalk," who missed his number being called and had to start all over. The Bureau was filled that day with the joyful of heart and sorrowful of soul.

Proverbs 14:10 (NLT) says, *"Each heart knows its own bitterness, and no one else can fully share its joy."* Scripture explains that we can witness the actions of others without fully understanding the feelings and emotions surrounding those actions. Although I couldn't completely understand the sorrow and joy of those at the Driver's Licence Bureau, on some level I could rejoice with my new gal pal, feel bad for "Mr. Sleeping on the Sidewalk," and have compassion for the determined elderly gentleman.

I was reminded that day that though my understanding is limited, I serve an all-knowing God who can completely understand each heart's sorrow and joy.

week 12 reflections

1. 1. Take a few moments and reread this devotional. We quickly make judgments about others as we go through our days, but only God fully understands the hearts of those around us. Think about someone in your neighborhood, church, workplace, or other group whom you don't know very well. What thoughts or judgments have you mentally made about that person? Make a simple plan to get to know that person better.

2. Think about the three people specifically mentioned in this devotional. Which person did you have the most compassion for? Why? What words could you have spoken to that person to encourage him or her?

3. Proverbs has often been referred to as "Life's Little Instruction Manual." Because there are 31 chapters in the book of Proverbs, this would be a great "daily read," reading one chapter each day for a month. Why is the wisdom in Proverbs so important to our Christian walk?

4. Each of us has lived through times of sorrow and times of joy. In your own life, think of one special "time of joy." Write a short prayer praising God for this experience.

13 *Breath of God*

I've heard the oxygen mask instructions from flight attendants on a number of occasions.

"In the event that air pressure changes in the cabin and oxygen is required, a mask will automatically appear. Rest assured that though the mask may not be inflated that oxygen is flowing. Please place the mask over your nose and mouth, adjusting the elastic straps to fit tightly around your head. If you are traveling with a child, or someone who needs assistance with his or her mask, please make sure your own mask is in place before assisting someone else."

The emotional side of me wonders, if someone was sitting next to me struggling to breathe, would I be able to attend to my own needs before helping my loved one, friend, or even a stranger. The practical side of me understands that if I don't have proper oxygen that I may become incapacitated and unable to help, but the emotional side of me wonders what choice I would make.

In Revelation chapter 2, John was writing about the church at Ephesus. *"I know what you do, how you work hard and never give up. I know you do not put up with the false teachings of evil people...You have patience and have suffered troubles for my name and have not given up. But I have this against you: You have left the love you had in the beginning."* Revelation 2:2-4 (NCV)

He praised them for their hard work, tenacity, discernment, patience, and sufferings for the Gospel, but he also corrected them for not giving the LORD the proper place in their lives. They were hard workers, obviously busy with the work of God. They were people of morality and character. It appears, however, that in their time-consuming service for the Kingdom, they neglected their relationship with the King of the Kingdom.

They were busy putting oxygen masks on everyone around them, while neglecting their own need for air. Eventually they would become incapacitated and unable to help. Serving and helping others is wonderful, but as we serve, let's be purposeful in breathing in the presence of God into our lives; loving Jesus and maintaining a right relationship with Him must be foremost in how we live.

week 13 reflections

1. If you have flown in a commercial airplane, you have heard (and perhaps ignored) these instructions about the oxygen masks. As you read these instructions in the context of this devotional, what thoughts came to mind?

2. Revelation author, John, shares Jesus' impressions about the church at Ephesus, including both compliments and rather severe criticism. Have you recognized the important work of your own church that made you feel good about its care and outreach? List your compliments about your church.

3. Have you attended a church where you were concerned that the focus was not on God's work or that the church had "lost its first love"? Summarize these concerns into a sentence or two.

4. God's requirements for His people are about their obedience, trust, and heart. Reread the first 4 commandments listed in the "Ten Commandments" (Exodus 20:1-17) and note your reactions to them.

14 A Hair-raising Experience

Every one of us on occasion has had a bad haircut. My stylist is wonderful, but every once in a while she focuses more on our conversation than actually cutting my hair, and I end up with a style that I didn't request. God asked the Prophet Ezekiel to give himself a new look.

"Now, son of man, take a sharp sword and use it as a barber's razor to shave your head and your beard. Then take a set of scales and divide up the hair. When the days of your siege come to an end, burn a third of the hair inside the city. Take a third and strike it with the sword all around the city. And scatter a third to the wind. For I will pursue them with drawn sword. But take a few hairs and tuck them away in the folds of your garment." Ezekiel 5:1~3 (NIV)

Once Ezekiel had his new style, he was to weigh his cut-off locks, and divide them into three parts: a third of the hair was to be burned, a third cut with a sword, and a third thrown to the wind. He was also to keep a few strands inside his clothing.

In Ezekiel's day, the hair symbolized what was in store for the people left in Jerusalem: a third of the people would die during the siege and burning of Jerusalem, another third would die at the hands of their enemy, and a third would be scattered into exile. The hair the prophet placed in his garment represented the faithful who had remained true to the LORD in face of dire circumstances.

Does Ezekiel's prophecy have merit for us today? And if so, how do we apply this passage of Scripture to our lives? I would like to focus on the strands of hair that Ezekiel placed among his clothing.

As women serving Jesus, we need to remember that in the midst of chaos and crisis, in times when the enemies of God appear to have the upper hand, there will always be a select group who remain faithful to spiritual truth. The LORD is moving in this earth. He is calling people to Himself, and we are privileged to be His servants who shed His light abroad.

May the LORD continue to use us mightily for His purposes. May our ministry efforts draw those who are being burned with fire, cut with the sword, and scattered to the wind into the faithful fold of God.

week 14 reflections

1. A bad haircut! We've all had one – or perhaps more than one!!! Why does the cut of our hair impact us so much?

2. At first read, this Scripture may not have meaning for our lives today. This devotional helps us understand this passage in Ezekiel. God was using the hair of Ezekiel to symbolize what was about to happen. Why do you think God used hair as a symbol?

3. When we hear news reports or see broadcasts about troubling events in our world, we sometimes are left shaking our heads and struggling to understand. But as we look back at Old Testament times, we realize some things haven't changed: violence, death, and destruction are still in our world. Why do you think it's this way?

4. We are encouraged to know that *"there will always be a select group who remain faithful to spiritual truth. The LORD is moving in this earth. He is calling people to Himself, and we are privileged to be His servants who shed His light abroad."* There is now – and always has been – a remnant of believers. How are you involved in fulfilling God's plan?

15 Ode to the Man in Brown

When I lived on the Eastern Plains of Colorado, the local UPS delivery man didn't like me. It all started when my two pet goats, Zeb and Zeke, climbed into the back of Mr. UPS' truck. The boys began to make mischief and couldn't be persuaded to return to their yard.

The man in brown had the nerve to call my adorable babies "aggressive." In truth, the twins were curious and at times naughty - but never aggressive. When the delivery driver complained, it was all I could do NOT to point out that Mr. FedEx and the local post lady, Ms. Marie, had not voiced any complaints. Of course, Ms. Marie delivered our mail a mile down the road, and Mr. FedEx had learned that the boys always enjoy a good dog treat.

An arrangement was made that the UPS man would throw any packages out his window onto the driveway. I quit having anything breakable delivered and all went well. In preparation for our move to Africa, Zeb and Zeke were given to my husband's co-worker. When Zeb and Zeke left for their new home, the man in brown began placing packages by the front door.

One evening during the Christmas season that year, as I was exiting our driveway for a fun evening with friends, Mr. UPS was waiting to enter the driveway. Wanting to extend an olive branch, I left my SUV and approached his truck.

"Good evening. I'm so sorry that you're working late," I spoke sincerely.

He was curt. He quickly gathered my package. "I've already put in twelve hours and I'm not done yet, but you have your package and that's all that's important, right?"

This was my moment to bridge a difficult situation. "No, that's not all that's important. Thank you for your service, but it's also important to me that both you and your family enjoy your Christmas." I could tell by the look on his face that my words surprised him. A verse in the Book of Proverbs as translated in the Christian Standard Bible says, *"When it is in your power, don't withhold good from the one to whom it belongs."* (Proverbs 3:27) If I were to paraphrase Proverbs 3:27 it would say something like this..., "If there is an opportunity for you to show God's love, kindness, and compassion, then you must be compelled to act accordingly." Every day there are opportunities to do good.

week 15 reflections

1. What was your reaction to this story?

2. There are many people involved in the "customer service" industry, including the delivery people mentioned in this devotional. Think about someone in this line of work who you interacted with recently. Explain the situation and your actions or thoughts.

3. Have you ever worked in the "customer service" industry? If so, summarize the difficulties you had dealing with the public.

4. The Hebrew translation of the phrase "is due" means "the owners of the good." The proverb says that a service provider who earns money, or learns a trade, or earns a word of honor or respect, this person should not have to wait for what belongs rightfully to him or her when it is within the power "meaning jurisdiction" of your person to give it. The verse avoids the question of whether you are the one who was served! Do you know of someone deserving of something you can provide? Maybe you are God's funnel of mercy or justice.

16 *Living and Giving*

I have heard it said a number of times that money is the root of all evil. Scripture actually says that the *"LOVE of money is the root of all evil."* 1 Timothy 6:10 (paraphrased) The word "love" used in this verse is a unique Greek word. It actually means to have friendship with coin or silver. In 1 Timothy, one of Paul's Pastoral Epistles, he describes how friendship with money can cause harm to individuals and to the church at large. Paul discusses how being closely knit with money will lead to false doctrines, controversies, envy, strife, malicious talk, evil suspicions, and constant friction. The Apostle even says that some people, because of their relationship with money, have pierced themselves with many griefs.

I recently had an interesting experience at a Walmart store in Colorado. I had dropped Chris off at a friend's place of business and was "buying time" before picking him up. I was browsing through the socks department, when I noticed a young woman frantically crawling on the floor. She was looking for some money that had fallen out of her pocket. Given the unsanitary conditions of the floor, I assumed that she had misplaced a fairly large amount of money. I almost jokingly asked if there was a reward before joining her in the quest for lost treasure. While looking under a rack of sleep shirts, she mentioned that the missing four dollars was a co-payment for her child's prescription. She obviously didn't have any more money, and I was blessed that day to give my new friend a five-dollar bill.

Over the last couple weeks, I have had a "money situation" come up with a ministry friend. One of those kinds of situations that – if not kept in check – can cause, like Paul indicated in Scripture, controversy, strife, suspicions, and friction. It was easy to give $5 to a friend at Walmart, but I have been challenged lately about my attitude toward money when the amount exceeds a few dollars.

I do not want a friendship with money. How odd to imagine myself hugging or kissing my wallet! I want money to be a tool in my life; a tool for living and a tool for giving. My husband and I purposed a number of years ago to own our possessions and not have them own us. I don't want any possession or amount of money in my life to be so important that I couldn't freely give it away if God asked.

week 16 reflections

1. Read 1 Timothy 6:10. Write this Scripture in your own words. Add a sentence or two expanding this thought as it fits into today's culture.

2. Have you ever had a *"friendship with coin or silver"*? Explain the situation and what happened.

3. As we see others who are less fortunate, either in other countries, or right in our own neighborhood, we recognize that money can give us options. Describe your relationship with money, including options that money allows in your life.

4. In this devotional, the author recognizes the need to *"own our possessions and not have them own us."* What change in thinking or spending does this commitment cause one to make?

17 The Pot of Death

Elisha was a prophet who returned to Gilgal during a time of famine in that region. I believe that he returned to Gilgal knowing there was a famine in the land. He was not intimidated to travel to a place where there was a lack of food. In fact, he may have viewed the dire circumstances of this region as an opportunity to see the hand of God move in a miraculous way. *"While the Guild of Prophets were having a meal with him, he instructed his attendant, 'Put a large pot on the fire and boil some stew for the Guild of Prophets.' Somebody went out into the fields to grab some herbs, found a wild vine, and gathered a lap full of wild gourds, which he came and sliced up into the stew pot, but nobody else knew. When they served the men, they began to eat the stew. But they cried out, 'That pot of stew is deadly, you man of God!' So they couldn't eat the stew. But he replied, 'Bring me some flour.' He tossed it into the pot and said, 'Serve the people so they can eat.' Then there was nothing harmful in the pot."* 2 Kings 4:38-41 (ISV) The name "Gilgal" means rolling or moving. God wanted to move or do something amazing in a desolating place.

When people are desperate, they do desperate things. The servant, who was given the task of feeding the prophets, knowingly gathered gourds from a wild vine. The original Hebrew text indicates that this vine was prolific. It produced seemingly great bounty. I have read reports of people, because of extreme hunger, eating dirt, straw or grass. My husband and I watched a documentary a couple years ago about a young man struggling to survive through the winter in a remote part of Alaska. When spring arrived, due to extreme hunger and desperation, he ate poisonous berries. Judgment is often impaired when people are destitute.

Food was scarce in Gilgal. It is interesting that the company of prophets instantly recognized their plight and looked to Elisha for help. Divinely inspired, he added flour to the stew, making it fit for consumption.

I believe we shouldn't be afraid to visit places where there is famine and where people may lack good judgment because of it. We need to remember that desperate people may not have good judgment. We need to sense when there is trouble or "death in the pot." When called upon for help, we need to rely on God for wisdom and direction, and what other people see as "waste" might be in our hands of ministry a means of provision. We should view the lack as an opportunity for God to do something amazing because of His sovereignty over everything, and because of His love.

week 17 reflections

1. This story in 2 Kings is an unusual one. Reread it and write a summary of what happened in your own words.

2. *"When people are desperate, they do desperate things."* Think of a time when you were desperate, or someone you know or have heard of was desperate. What irrational or unusual thing did you – or that person – do?

3. God wants us to call on Him for provision. *"When called upon for help, we need to rely on God for wisdom and direction."* This isn't always our first thought in times of trouble. Consider a time when you were in need and called upon God for help. What happened?

4. How can this story in 2 Kings be applied to our daily life? Write a "proverb" to help you remember the main point of this event.

18 *Lamenting*

Lamentations is a book of poetry, one poem per chapter. *"My eyes will flow unceasingly, until the LORD looks down from heaven and sees. What I see brings grief to my soul because of all the women in my city."* Lamentation 3:49-51 (NIV) The words express grief at the horror and bitterness of what had happened in Jerusalem. The author of Lamentations, possibly Jeremiah, sees the destruction that the Babylonian army has brought to the city. He does not mince words when describing the terror that has befallen God's people. He acknowledges that the LORD's judgment has come to Israel, but he also remembers God's compassion, *"Though he brings grief, he will show compassion, so great is his unfailing love, for he does not willingly bring affliction or grief to anyone."* Lamentations 3:32-33 (NIV)

The King James Version of Lamentations 3:51 says, *"Mine eye affecteth mine heart because of all the daughters of my city."* Jeremiah saw the devastation experienced by the daughters of the LORD, in his community in particular, and was moved to tears. There have been times in my life when I have been unwilling to "look". I remember being on Pine Ridge Reservation a number of years ago prayer walking with a team of ladies in a rough neighborhood. We were standing outside an abandoned building asking the LORD to intervene in the lives of the Lakota people. In the midst of our prayers, loud voices overwhelmed us, and sounds of someone running came from what we thought was a vacant warehouse! A couple of the ladies peered through the broken windows to see what was taking place – but I couldn't bring myself to look. I didn't want to see.

God has called us to "look" at the destruction in our world. As Christian women, we must look and allow what we see to affect our hearts. When Jeremiah looked, he was moved with compassion. If we just have knowledge, but don't see for ourselves, instead of compassion we might experience judgment. Jeremiah knew that God had lifted His hand of blessing. All around us we can see the devastation of sin, but, like Jeremiah, we need to remember that God will show compassion because of His great unfailing love.

As Christian women, we must look and allow what we see to affect our hearts. In turn, we must pray and do something to bring about change.

week 18 reflections

1. This Scripture from Lamentations is a sad one. No one wants to think about the horrors of the history of Jerusalem. Read the entire chapter of Lamentations 3 and summarize what happened in a few sentences.

2. Why do you think there is so much terror, war, disease, and grief in the world?

3. *"God has called us to 'look' at the destruction in our world."* What destruction or evil do you see happening in today's world?

4. This devotion ends with a challenge: *"As Christian women, we must look and allow what we see to affect our hearts. In turn, we must pray and do something to bring about change."* What specific things can you do to bring about change in the world?

19 *Being a Sound*

Water is very symbolic in Scripture. The Book of John compares water to eternal life in Jesus. *"…'Everyone drinking of this water will thirst again; but whoever may drink of the water that I will give him will never thirst, to the age. Instead, the water that I will give to him will become in him a spring of water, welling up into eternal life.'"* John 4:13-14 (BLB)

Also in the Book of John, water references the Holy Spirit flowing through believers. *"If anyone thirsts, let him come to Me and drink. The one believing in Me, as the Scripture has said: 'Out of his belly will flow rivers of living water.'"* John 7:37-38 (BLB)

As a middle school student, I remember learning about the different types of bodies of water. The one that confused me was a sound - a long wide body of water connecting larger bodies of water, wider and deeper than a channel (Merriam-Webster Dictionary). In my young mind, "sound" was something a person made and heard, not a description of water. My older mind, however, enjoys the play on words. I want to be a sound (a conduit of the Holy Spirit) to sound (make noise and be heard) the truths of God. I want streams of living water to flow through me.

There is no hope for people outside of having a personal relationship with Christ. He is the living water. Those who drink of His salvation will never thirst again. We are called to be ministers of mercy, sharing spiritual truths and providing for physical needs. We need to help those lacking natural water here on earth, but more importantly, we need to share about the well of eternal life. God wants us to be a stream of living water where the Holy Spirit anoints and uses us to impact hurting women and children.

God wants to use us to do something creative and important in our world. I believe that all over the earth, God is using women as conduits for His work. His Spirit is flowing through believers. The Word of God is reaching peoples, multitudes, and nations.

The next time we drink a glass of water from a faucet, sip from bottled water, shower, or take a dip in a pool, let's remind ourselves of God's great calling to be living water.

week 19 reflections

1. Water is essential to life. List at least 10 ways you use water in your daily life.

2. Read John 4:1-30 about the encounter of Jesus with the Samaritan woman. What was the "living water" that Jesus referred to?

3. Water is life! Without water, life ceases. Think about not watering your indoor plants, or what happens when there is a lack of rain on a farm. No water – no life! In what specific ways can we be "living water"?

4. We can serve God by being a "sound" - a long wide body of water connecting larger bodies of water. How can you be a "sound" in your church, Bible class, small group, or neighborhood?

20 Thirty Sayings of the Wise

I wish I could say that I wake up every morning eager to read my Bible and pray. I generally wake up thinking about all the tasks that need to be done that day. I have found that if I don't begin my day by spending time with the LORD that somehow night comes, and I have neglected what is most important.

One of my favorite Bible passages is Proverbs 22, 23, and 24. These verses in my Bible have the title, "Thirty Sayings of the Wise." When I read Proverbs, I am challenged to live rightly. Time and time again the Book of Proverbs calls us to listen. *"Listen to the words of the wise; apply your heart to my instruction. For it is good to keep these sayings in your heart and always ready on your lips. I am teaching you today—yes, you—so you will trust in the Lord. I have written thirty sayings for you, filled with advice and knowledge."* Proverbs 22:17-20 (NLT)

Listed below are the thirty sayings of wisdom:

1. Be kind to the poor.
2. Choose your friends wisely.
3. Don't be responsible for another's debt.
4. Be respectful toward previous generations.
5. Work hard allowing God to prosper.
6. Have self-control.
7. There are things more important than money.
8. Always be generous.
9. Be receptive to advice.
10. Be fair in business practices.
11. Listen carefully.
12. Discipline your children.
13. Rejoice when children make good decisions.
14. Fear the LORD – don't envy sinners.
15. Discipline is necessary.
16. Listen to, be respectful to your parents.
17. Promiscuity is dangerous.
18. Don't overindulge in alcohol.
19. Evil people are not good associates.
20. Let wisdom be your foundation.
21. There is strength in wisdom.
22. Lead others with wisdom.
23. Fools experience alienation.
24. Wisdom brings self-control and strength.
25. Prevent injustice and suffering.
26. Wisdom is sweet like honey.
27. Setbacks are opportunities to grow.
28. Love your enemies.
29. The prosperity of the wicked is fleeting.
30. Remain honest about all things.

week 20 reflections

1. Read Proverbs 22, 23, and 24. What is important about these chapters?

2. Select one of the thirty sayings of the wise and write it here. Why did this one seem to "jump out" at you?

3. All of these sayings are good to remember. Could you cluster them into categories? List the categories you've chosen and then place the numbers of the sayings that belong in each category.

4. Select one of these sayings that you're struggling with in your life. Draw a picture or cartoon to help you remember the wisdom of this saying.

21 Who's the "Boss"?

Chris and I have some dear friends who have a son about four years old. Often their young boy asks, "Who's the boss?" It appears to be very important to him to understand who is in charge. As spiritual women, likewise, it is important to assess who's in charge.

In 1 Samuel 13, Saul and his troops were waiting to attack the Philistines. Prior to the Israelites going into battle, the Prophet Samuel was supposed to come and sacrifice offerings to the LORD. Scripture tells us, *"Saul waited there seven days for Samuel... but Samuel still didn't come... So he demanded, 'Bring me the burnt offering and the peace offerings!' And Saul sacrificed the burnt offering himself. Just as Saul was finishing with the burnt offering, Samuel arrived. Saul went out to meet and welcome him, but Samuel said, 'What is this you have done?' Saul replied, '...I felt compelled to offer the burnt offering before you came.'"* 1 Samuel 13:8-12 (NLT) Saul took matters into his own hands and made the offering himself. Saul was a natural leader. He was charismatic and had a strong personality. He wasn't afraid to make difficult decisions. He wasn't fearful of battle and certainly knew how to lead his men. Saul, however, didn't understand that there were occasions where he wasn't in charge; he wasn't the boss.

When we step outside of our boundaries and take matters into our own hands, we can become offensive to others, and we can, also, like Saul, become offensive to God.

When we first moved to South Africa, I had to ask myself, on a number of occasions, what operating outside of my boundaries looked like. I was in someone else's backyard, and until our ministry was established, I had no business operating in an authoritative capacity. I came up with these items to guide me in knowing my boundaries:

1. If I am not in charge, I shouldn't act like I'm in charge. I don't interrupt, ask too many questions, or even offer my opinion unless I am asked.

2. I don't have my own agenda. My agenda is subject to the person in charge.

3. Even if the person in charge is struggling and others are looking for me to make decisions, I do not usurp someone else's authority.

4. I am not critical - privately or publicly - about someone else's leadership.

May we operate inside the boundaries that the LORD has given us.

week 21 reflections

1. Summarize the essence of the situation in 1 Samuel 13:8-12.

2. *"Saul, along with his men, became impatient waiting for Samuel to arrive. Saul took matters into his own hands and made the offering himself."* Impatience is a trait of many of us. Remember a time when your impatience caused a problem or unpleasant situation and explain what happened.

3. "Who's the boss?" is an important question as we go through each day. Good or bad, think about "who's the boss?" in your own family and how the answer makes you feel.

4. Read through the list of guidelines listed in the devotional. Which of these resonates with you? Why?

22 *Womb Cleansing*

When Chris and I first arrived in South Africa we stayed with some dear friends in the town of Rustenburg. Our friends were extremely hospitable. They opened their home to us like we were family, and were instrumental in helping us acquire a car, open new bank accounts, purchase cell phones, obtain insurance, and accomplish numerous other requirements needed to help us navigate our ministry transition to Africa.

A few days after we arrived, we went shopping in the center of their small town. A piece of luggage had been lost in our travels, and we were on a quest to purchase pants for Chris. The area we were in was nothing like anything I had ever seen in America, and I was curious about everything. Chris had to keep telling me to pay attention and to keep up with our friends who were guiding us.

I noticed signage on almost every street post that said, "Womb Cleansing." I couldn't help but stop and read what the posts were about. It didn't take long for me to understand, even with somewhat of a language barrier, that the signs were advertisements for abortion clinics.

I understand that abortion is common in most parts of the world, but I had never heard of the procedure being called "womb cleansing." The loss of life is heartbreaking to me, and if possible, my heart broke a little more when I realized the deceptiveness of the terminology being used. *"As you know not what is the way of the wind, nor how the bones do grow in the womb of her that is with child: even so you know not the works of God who makes all."* Ecclesiastes 11:5 (KJV2000) Life is sacred. Only God understands how a baby grows in the womb of a mother.

I am always careful when I address the issue of abortion. Babies are harmed and so are the women who have made this difficult decision. I want to speak the truth about the taking of life, and I also want to be sensitive to women who are struggling with the aftermath of abortion.

As Christian women, individually and corporately, may we always stand for life: physical life and spiritual life, because God is an amazing God, who forms all things.

week 22 reflections

1. Ecclesiastes 11:5 is a powerful Scripture. Rewrite this in your own words.

2. This is a sensitive subject, but God Himself creates life. He alone maintains the right to life giving and taking. What was your reaction to the "womb cleansing" signs in South Africa?

3. Focus on "the deceptiveness of the terminology" for the abortion signs. Why does the wording matter?

4. Abortion is a difficult topic to discuss with women. Think about how you would respond if someone mentions she has had an abortion, and write it here:

23 Are You My Mother?

I love Africa. The landscape, people, and, of course, the wildlife are all amazing. Chris, my husband, also places himself in the category of wildlife, so how can I not be amazed by the creatures who reside here?

I keep learning from Africa. Take zebras for instance. When a baby is born, the mother isolates the new life from the rest of the herd. The baby can only see the stripes or markings of the mother. He or she is not exposed to the uniqueness of the other animals in the herd. The mother will often simply stare at the baby. Observers believe the idea is that the baby and mother learn to instantly distinguish each other from other zebras.

Zebras also bite each other. Sometimes they bite as a form of affection, and sometimes they bite as a form of aggression. Either way, whether a gentle nibble or piercing grip, zebras have no trouble communicating their thoughts to one another.

Living in a foreign country has its challenges. Without realizing it, I am constantly making a fool of myself. At first everything was new and different here – including shopping, traveling, how instructions are given, and how people are greeted. As I've become more immersed in the culture, things don't seem as strange, but there are still struggles. Because I can't rely on the familiar, I find myself continually asking the LORD to guide me and give me understanding and wisdom.

Although my situation overseas is a little unique, I believe that if we permit the LORD, He will place each and every one of us in unusual circumstances. He will put us in places that are unfamiliar, so we are forced to rely on the leading of the Holy Spirit.

We need to be like the zebras. It is important that we spend time in God's presence – simply staring at Him. When we understand more about the LORD, it is easier to recognize Him. Our eyes should be constantly searching, looking for the one we love. In the midst of the crowd, we should know and clearly see our Savior.

week 23 reflections

1. Why do you think zebra mothers isolate their young?

2. Have you ever been in an unfamiliar and uncomfortable situation? Summarize how you felt.

3. How do you stay close to God?

4. How would your days be different if you stayed focused on God and allowed the Holy Spirit to lead you each day?

24 Let the Children Come

Chris and I recently attended a small church service outside of the City of Rustenburg. The chapel was beautiful and the setting surrounding the facility was lovely. It was still winter in South Africa, but the roses were blossoming and the shrubbery greening. We could see the mountains in the distance. The day was warm, and the sun was shining brightly. We were greeted with handshakes and embraces and certainly felt most welcome. The church was only a couple months old. We praised and worshipped together singing with a CD. There was a sweet presence of the LORD in His house that morning.

During the pastor's message, he became distracted by his young son. The boy had left children's church and marched up the center aisle of the adult chapel looking for his toy car. The child was approximately four years old and very determined. He approached the front left-hand side set of pews, where he had previously sat with his mother, and began his search. The mom, of course, was trying to hush him and escort him back to the other children. After a couple moments, the pastor simply stated, "I apologize, but I am distracted by my boy." He then questioned what was wrong with his son, the toy car was found, and the lad headed back down the center aisle with the toy in his chubby hand.

I was moved by the pastor's attention to his son. I know that some would see the young boy's actions as disruptive and criticize the parents for not taking control more quickly, but, in my mind, the pastor was doing what a father does best – attending to the needs of his child. In Scripture, Jesus placed great importance on children who at that time of life have very little clue of important things. *"One day some parents brought their children to Jesus so he could lay his hands on them and pray for them. But the disciples scolded the parents for bothering them. But Jesus said, 'Let the children come to me. Don't stop them! For the Kingdom of Heaven belongs to those who are like these children.' And he placed his hands on their heads and blessed them before he left."* Matthew 19:13-15 (NLT)

One of the things that I truly enjoy about our ministry in South Africa is the importance that we place on helping children. May the LORD bless our hands to pray and tend to the needs of children all over the world.

week 24 reflections

1. Our lives are filled with distractions. The pastor in this story allowed himself to be distracted by his son, and then he was able to continue with his work. What was your reaction to this story?

2. Why do distractions seem so infuriating? What can we learn from the pastor's acknowledgment of his son?

3. Why do you think Jesus placed great importance on children?

4. In what ways do you positively impact the lives of children?

25 Into Every Life a Little Snake Must Crawl

A number of weeks ago, Salome, the young woman who helps in our home in South Africa, found a snake in the bottom of the master bedroom closet. Chris and I had just returned from Tanzania, so the house had set vacant for a couple of weeks. In our absence, a cobra had come indoors and made himself comfortable. Two of our landlord's workers quickly arrived and sent Mr. Cobra to heaven. If snakes go to heaven. I'm not sure. I know the saying, "All dogs go to heaven," but I've never heard the same said of snakes. Elvis and Johann, the snake killing heroes, put the cobra in a bucket. Even in death, the body of the snake kept moving. It was a sight to behold!

Chris had returned from Tanzania very ill. He was running an extremely high temperature and taking a number of strong medications. Several hours later, when I carried the snake bucket into the guest room, where Chris was resting, he responded in his delirium, "Into every life a little snake must crawl."

Later that day, I googled snakes and learned that a cobra can kill an elephant with one bite. The cobra in our home was approximately five feet long. I was able to measure it because as a souvenir Elvis and Johann returned the hide to me.

I'm not sure where to place the snake skin in our home. It doesn't seem to fit with my usual decorating style, but then again nothing has been "usual" about my life since moving to Africa. I do know, however, that Chris and I have agreed to put "our cobra" on display as a testimony to God's fame. His love and protection are truly great!

Psalm 102:12 (NLT) says, *"But you, O LORD, will sit on your throne forever. Your fame will endure to every generation."* Verse 18 of the same psalm says that the famous deeds of God should be a record for future generations, so that people not yet born will praise Him.

"Into every life a little snake must crawl." Please be encouraged this week that God is preparing to rescue and help you in your time of breath-taking fear. When troubles come, remember that God is the Famous One.

week 25 reflections

1. How do you feel about snakes? What would your reaction have been to find a cobra in your bedroom closet?

2. Read through Psalm 102. What insights did you gain about God?

3. *"…the famous deeds of God should be a record for future generations, so that people not yet born will praise Him."* Why is this important?

4. God is famous! Jesus lived 2,000 years ago, and yet this one-word name is recognized throughout the world. Translators are busy translating God's Word into languages and tongues in every nation. Soon all will be able to read God's Word and know of His Righteousness. Why do you think just the mention of the name of "Jesus" either draws or repels people?

26 The Road Less Traveled

A good friend of mine recently shared a story about getting lost. She was visiting a mutual girlfriend who lives in California. The two, along with a third friend, were driving to Coronado Island. They realized too late that they were headed in the wrong direction. There was no place to turn around, and they ended up in Mexico. My friend is a great story teller. I could picture her frustration in navigating Tijuana and then trying to re-enter the U.S. without proper documentation. The Bible tells us that there is a way that seems right to man, but that in the end what appears to be right is actually the wrong path to travel. (Proverbs 16:25) On numerous occasions in my life, I have done things that appear right in the moment, but in the end they were actually wrong. I recently made a ministry decision that in hindsight was not the right way to go. I made the decision based on pleasing others and trying to keep peace. At the time, I felt frantic to keep everything afloat. In actuality, I should have let things fall apart and relied on God to guide my travels.

I have always enjoyed Robert Frost's poem about the road less traveled.

"I shall be telling this with a sigh, somewhere ages and ages hence:
Two roads diverged in a wood, and I took the one less traveled by,
and that has made all the difference."

It reminds me of my spiritual journey. Often in my walk here on earth, roads have diverged, and I've been challenged to choose a path. In Mr. Frost's insightful poem, he describes the path chosen as grassy and wanting wear.

As women in ministry, the roads we travel are often in need of wear. They've been neglected and unused for far too long. They are covered with grasses and their destinations can be difficult to discern.

We need to be mindful that the less traveled roads that we walk "make all the difference." We are changed by our journey, and those we meet along the way are, likewise, changed. Their lives on earth, and hopefully for eternity are altered by our voices of truth, our prayers, and the love and kindness that emits from our hands of service. May the LORD continue to guide us and lead us on the road less traveled.

week 26 reflections

1. Google the poem, "The Road Not Taken," by Robert Frost, and read it. Or go to: www.poetryfoundation.org/resources/learning/core-poems/detail/44272 and listen to the poem being read. What are your impressions?

2. Think about times in your life when you had two choices and had to make a decision. Summarize the choices, your decision, and your reasoning.

3. Ponder the decision and reasoning you listed. Do you have any regrets? Would you do anything different if you had to make the choice today? Why or why not?

4. *"We are changed by our journey, and those we meet along the way are, likewise, changed."* What part of your journey with God changed you forever? Were others affected? Share your thoughts.

27 Does God Know How to Tie Shoes?

I recently came across a children's book entitled, "Does God Know How to Tie Shoes?" by Nancy White Carlstrom. The book reminded me of a long-term substitute teaching assignment that I had a few years ago. In first grade, shoe-tying is a milestone. Ask a six- or seven-year-old and he or she will tell you that tying shoes isn't for the faint of heart. Different techniques work for different students. There's the "rabbit through the hole" scenario, the two loop method, and the one loop skill involving the wrap-around. There is also the famous "I'm not ready to tie my own shoes; I need help" technique.

My husband grew up in Chicago and as a child was a friend with two first cousins, a boy and a girl. The two cousins were in the same first grade classroom. When entering first grade the girl already knew how to tie her shoes, but the boy did not. Each day as shoes were changed for P.E. class, the girl would quickly tie her own shoes and then race to her cousin's side to provide the needed help.

Matthew 25 tells us that whatever we do for the least, we do unto God. In the Greek, the least is described as someone small in stature. On the surface that would mean children but on a deeper level, Scripture is also talking about others who need assistance: the impoverished, the heartbroken, the lost, the sick in body, the discouraged, and the depressed. Difficult seasons of life can make us feel small.

While teaching first grade, I enjoyed shoe-tying moments with the children. There was something special about kneeling before a child and tying his shoes. Sometimes the student would place her foot on my knee. I would bend slightly and entwine the laces. Being in close proximity was the perfect opportunity to share a smile, a private joke, or a word of encouragement.

Does God know how to tie shoes? I believe He does, and as His servants, I also believe that He has anointed us to tie shoes. Is our ministry responsibility always easy? No – there are knotted laces, dirty shoes, and smelly feet. Yet there is such joy in helping the least of these. Happy tying! Remember Velcro is for wimps!

week 27 reflections

1. Many children never experience the challenge of "shoe-tying" today. Their parents have eluded the struggle by buying Velcro or slip-on types of shoes. What are your thoughts about children avoiding this skill?

2. Jesus talks about serving "the least of these" in Matthew 25:39-40 (CEB). The disciples asked: *"When did we see you sick or in prison and visit you?' Then the king will reply to them, 'I assure you that when you have done it for one of the least of these brothers and sisters of mine, you have done it for me.'"* We are all called to serve "the least of these." Share about a time when you served.

3. "Difficult seasons of life can make us feel small." Reflect on a time when you "felt small." What was happening in your life at that time?

4. We all need to have someone focus on us and *"be in close proximity."* Who in your life fulfills that need for you? Are you fulfilling that need for someone?

28 *Picking a Fight*

"One day Jonathan said to his armor-bearer, 'Come on, let's go over to where the Philistines have their outpost…' To reach the Philistine outpost, Jonathan had to go down between two rocky cliffs that were called Bozez and Seneh. 'Let's go across to the outpost of those pagans,' Jonathan said to his armor-bearer. 'Perhaps the Lord will help us, for nothing can hinder the Lord. He can win a battle whether he has many warriors or only a few!' …When the Philistines saw them coming, they shouted… 'Come on up here, and we'll teach you a lesson!' 'Come on, climb right behind me,' Jonathan said to his armor-bearer, 'for the Lord will help us defeat them!' So they climbed up using both hands and feet, and the Philistines fell before Jonathan, and his armor-bearer killed those who came behind them…And just then an earthquake struck, and everyone was terrified."* In this passage, 1 Samuel 14:1-15 (NLT), Jonathan deliberately picks a fight with the Philistines. There are times when it is entirely appropriate to pick a fight. The Philistines, time and time again, were brutal bullies who oppressed God's people. Jonathan, the son of King Saul, decides to take a closer look at the Philistine camp. Sometimes all that is needed to stir us to fight is taking a closer look. Jonathan makes the decision to view the outpost without telling anyone other than his armor bearer. Looking closely at our enemies can be lonely and difficult. I love Jonathan's heartfelt attitude, *"Perhaps the LORD will help us, for nothing can hinder the LORD. He can win a battle whether He has many warriors or only a few!"*

When Jonathan observed his enemies, he understood that being moved emotionally wasn't enough. He needed to hear from God. Hearing from the LORD was risky; Jonathan and his friend had to stand in plain sight of the enemy. They allowed themselves to become targets on behalf of justice. It is interesting that they were between two rocky cliffs called Bozez and Seneh; words which together mean "slippery slope." When Jonathan received confirmation from the LORD, he and his armor bearer began to climb. The climb was so steep that they crawled on their hands and knees. The two fought and killed twenty Philistines while doing the belly crawl over half an acre! Panic broke out, the earth shook, and everyone was terrified. 1 Samuel 14:16 says that the vast army of the Philistines began to melt away in every direction. There are so many valuable truths in Jonathan's story: 1) while viewing injustice can move us emotionally, we also have to be moved spiritually; 2) ministry can make us a target; 3) fighting in mud while doing the army crawl is a valuable skill; 4) God can win with just a few, and, of course; 5) don't be afraid to pick a fight.

week 28 reflections

1. This story in 1 Samuel 14:1-15 showcases Jonathan's dedication to the LORD. What about this story stirs you?

2. *"As spiritual women, there are times when it is entirely appropriate for us to pick a fight."* Has there been a time in your life when you had to "pick a fight"? Summarize the scenario and your actions.

3. This is a great quote to remember: *"Perhaps the LORD will help us, for nothing can hinder the LORD. He can win a battle whether he has many warriors or only a few!"* What battle are you currently engaged in that needs God's help?

4. Explain which of the 5 "truths" speaks to you in your present situation?

29 *What Is His Name?*

AS Christians, we are commanded by God to share our faith. I believe we share the love of God both with our service and with our speech. As a child, I remember singing, "Tell Me the Story of Jesus." The lyrics still ring true today, *"Tell me the story of Jesus. Write on my heart every word. Tell me the story most precious, sweetest that ever was heard."* Frances J. Crosby

My husband and I recently met a young man. He appeared to be a Zimbabwean refugee, but we're not sure. We had some communication issues. He didn't speak English or Afrikaans (except to say "dankie" which means "thank you"). He was extremely thin and not very tall. He was perhaps 14 or 15 years of age. A number of his teeth were missing. His eyes and cheeks were sunken in, and his skin had a grayish tint from malnourishment. His clothes were ragged and torn, and he desperately needed a bath.

Chris and I were visiting a crafters mart in the town of Bela Bela, which is located about an hour and a half from our home. I use the words "crafters mart" loosely. The artisans display wares in a long tin-roofed shack with mostly open sides. The stalls are separated by faded cloths of varying colors. Our new friend was working there as a "car watcher" of sorts. He didn't seem to have the energy to solicit his services but made an attempt at directing us from our parking space. Chris held up his index finger motioning for the young man to stay put while we went and purchased some food for him. The love of Christ was shared through the nourishment we gave him, and our hand gestures: Chris pointed toward heaven and I placed my right hand over my heart.

The first several verses of Proverbs 30 describe the author's search for God.

"Who has gone up to heaven and come down? Who has gathered the wind in His hands?
Who has bound up the waters in a cloak?
Who has established all the ends of the earth?
What is His name, and what is the name of His Son—if you know?"
Proverbs 30:4 (HCSB)

The author understands that God is very powerful. He talks about the LORD holding the wind and wrapping the ocean in His cloak, but the writer wants to know God's name and the name of His son. The name "Bela Bela" means "beautiful". Who have you shared His beautiful name with today? Are you willing to share His name each and every day?

week 29 reflections

1. Reread Proverbs 30:4. Have you ever had questions about God or His son? What questions would you like answered about God?

2. Jesus said in Matthew 26:11 (BSB), *"The poor you will always have with you, but you will not always have me."* In every society, on every continent, there are "the poor." We cannot touch the great need of all the poor, but we can each do something. In what specific ways can you "touch the poor"?

3. Sharing the "beautiful name of God and the name of His son" can change lives. Think about and summarize a ministry or outreach or church you are involved in, and how they share the "beautiful name of God and the name of His son."

4. Children are filled with questions about God and Jesus. Ask a child you know about the questions he or she has and list them here. Are you able to give answers to these questions in a way that makes sense to the child?

30 Don't Intimidate Timothy

Scripture portrays young Timothy as an amazing pastor. He was a protégé of the Apostle Paul. God used Timothy in a great way to teach and pastor the early New Testament churches. Paul told Timothy not to despise his youth.

Paul also told the Corinthian Church not to intimidate Timothy. Why would the Church at Corinth want to intimidate Timothy? Did the leaders think they knew more than this young man in ministry? Did they resent the fact that Paul didn't visit them himself but sent Timothy on his behalf? Were there older people in the congregation looking back on their lives with regret? Were people upset that someone so young was being used by God so powerfully in ministry? I don't really know.

I recently met a young man in ministry. He is in his early 20's and serves the LORD on staff at a church here in South Africa. God has opened numerous doors for him to minister to youth. He is also a very talented musician and graphic designer. I'm not sure why, but I had trouble connecting with him. Maybe I was distracted or he was distracted, perhaps it was the environment, or even the other people present.

One of the things that sprung from my recent encounter was a call to pray about up-and-coming ministers in my life. I believe as a result of that prayer, the LORD moved on my behalf. Chris and I soon after received an e-mail from two young women wanting to visit. They are currently in college and working on an awareness project involving African orphans. I'm already asking the LORD to give me insight, wisdom, and words of encouragement. I want these young women to leave Africa full of passion for God and for His service. As seasoned women in ministry, we have a responsibility to encourage those who are young in their service for God. In South Africa, there are a number of antelope that share a unique trait. When they walk, their hind feet automatically step in the footprints left by their front feet. Are we making our footprints plain and easy to follow? Are we helping those who come behind us? Are we encouraging those who are young to passionately serve our LORD? When we meet someone beginning her ministry journey are we speaking words of life over her, or making judgments and developing negative attitudes? May the LORD use all of us to help and encourage those who walk in our steps behind us!

week 30 reflections

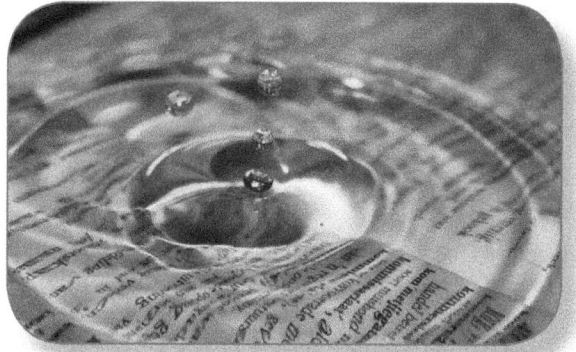

1. Why do you think the people in the Corinthian church would intimidate Timothy? Was it intentional?

2. Have you experienced a time when a younger person in ministry was not accepted as he or she should have been? Explain the situation.

3. There are times when the style of worship can become an issue in our churches. Younger people may have different ways of worshiping than older members of the church. This can cause friction. What do you think Paul would have said about this?

4. How can we encourage those who are young to passionately serve our LORD? What specific ideas do you have?

31

Droom
("Dream" in Afrikaans)

Chris and I recently attended an Afrikaans church in the town of Mokopane. The pastor was extremely gracious and for our benefit shared the key points of his sermon in English. His English was limited, so the congregation on occasion pitched in and helped with the translation.

On a bulletin board, in the sanctuary, was a large poster with the highlighted Afrikaans word "droom." As part of his message, the pastor shared the church's vision for the upcoming year and ways for the congregation to understand God's droom or dream for the church and for the individual lives represented.

Dreams are funny things. I recently had a dream about teaching school. I was standing in front of a class of third graders teaching a creative writing assignment. On the dry erase board located in front of the classroom, one of the students had drawn a green alien with wiry purple hair. As a class, we were building a character analysis, and the students were being very creative. We then moved forward in our lesson and designed a story web. I enjoyed my dream so much that I woke up laughing.

I also have dreams or aspirations for my life; some of those hopes center around ministry. I often pray about my dreams, asking God to help me, to guide me, and to open doors for me to further His work here on earth. I was challenged, however, by the "droom" poster in the Mokopane church. Am I so busy talking to the LORD about my dreams that I've neglected to seek Him about His dreams for me?

I've memorized a number of Scripture verses about God having a plan for my life, but I've never thought of His plan as actually being His dream for me. I am so moved that the Creator of the Universe has hopes, dreams, and aspirations for me. He wants to be the Dream Weaver of our lives.

In my sophomore year in high school, I attended the fall homecoming. The theme that year was "Dream Weaver." *"I just close my eyes again, and climb aboard the dream weaver train. Trying to take away my worries of the day and leave tomorrow behind. Dream weaver, I believe you can get me through the night. Dream weaver, I believe we can reach the morning night…"* Gary Wright

May the LORD "droomweave" for us, or weave His dream, into our lives.

week 31 reflections

1. A dream (or "droom") can seem very real and can infect our thoughts for days afterward. Consider a dream you've had recently and describe the content and its effect on you.

2. In our language, sometimes the word "dream" refers not to what happened in our mind as we slept, but refers to our vision, focus, or hope for our future. What dream have you had for your life that has either been accomplished or is one you are still hoping to achieve? Summarize it and your reactions to it.

3. What dreams or aspirations do you have for your children, your church, or an organization you're involved with?

4. In Scripture, we see that God has used dreams to direct the paths of His people. In the New Testament, Joseph had an angel appear to him in a dream, and Pilate's wife had a disturbing dream that she shared with her husband warning him not to "have anything to do with that innocent man" – referring to Jesus. Why do you think God uses dreams to share affirmations or instructions?

32 Beans, Beans, the Magical Fruit

Several summers ago, my mom and I took a mini vacation and drove to wild, wonderful West Virginia to visit family. My mom was not only focused on seeing the special people in her life but also about finding Mountain Half Runner Green Beans. These unique beans grow in the Appalachian hills, and, according to my mom, are a little taste of heaven on earth. We found the treasured beans at a vegetable stand along a narrow, winding, hilly road.

There's a story in the Bible about a man whose treasure was determined by a bean field. The last words of King David are found here. His words include a tribute to Shammah, one of David's elite warriors of his Mighty Men. *"…The Philistines gathered together at Lehi, where there was a plot of ground full of lentils, and the men fled from the Philistines. But he took his stand in the midst of the plot and defended it and struck down the Philistines, and the Lord worked a great victory."* 2 Samuel 23:11-12 (ESV) The name Shammah means "is there." In fact, in the Old Testament, one of the attributes of God is Jehovah-Shammah, which means "LORD is there." This mighty warrior experienced the presence of God with him in the bean field. His family was from Harar, which means "One-Who- Never-Sleeps".

The One Who Never Sleeps stood in the middle of the plot of ground and fought alongside Shammah. The Philistines were smug, ignorant, and arrogant people. Over and over again they harassed God's children.

The Israelite army fled but Shammah stood his ground. He was a man of substance. He was unwilling to part with the blessings of God. The bean field represents a coming harvest. The lentils would provide nourishment in the days ahead. The plot of land was given by God to His people, and Shammah was not going to walk away or run away from what God had given him.

As Christian women, we need to stand our ground. Even if we are standing alone, we need to remember that Jehovah-Shammah is there. Our God never sleeps. He is awake and attentive to our battles. In fact, He fights right beside us. We must be determined to see our spiritual harvest come to fruition. When we are harassed, we need to beat back our enemy and fight until we see the enemies of God defeated!

week 32 reflections

1. In this story, her mom had special memories of a food from her childhood - Mountain Half Runner Green Beans. Food can remind us of special times in our lives. What food from your childhood triggers a special memory? Why?

2. Read through 2 Samuel 23 and consider this story about David's Mighty Men. The Old Testament contains many stories of armies, warriors, and fighting. Why are these events significant parts of God's Word?

3. One of the many attributes of God is Jehovah-Shammah, which means "LORD is there." Sometimes it's hard to realize that God is actually with us in our trials. Think about a difficult time in your life where you now recognize that God was there with you. Summarize it and share your feelings.

4. Discrimination of believers happened throughout the times of the Bible, and continues to happen today, both in our lives and elsewhere. How can we *"pick up a jaw bone and fight until we see the enemies of God defeated"*?

33 Bras and Lavender

I have felt melancholy the past few days. I'm missing my girlfriends and the fellowship of other women. One of the hardest things about moving to a new location is the longing for friends left behind and the struggle, at times, to build new relationships.

Friendships of substance and depth don't happen overnight. Those kinds of relationships are built over the process of time. Sharing one's life with someone else isn't like watching a movie, where a plot, climax, and conclusion are all built and developed over a two-hour time frame. Great friendships are like a series of glimpses: past history, current circumstances, and dreams for the future viewed one segment at a time.

The Bible has a lot to say about friendships; coming first, is our relationship with our Creator, and second, relationships with one another. We need to choose our friends wisely. Scripture says that bad company corrupts good morals. We also need to choose friends who will challenge us. The Bible tells us that iron sharpens iron.

I once saw a greeting card that read, "Friends are like bras. You need to try them on in order to find the perfect fit." Since moving to South Africa, I've made several new friends. I haven't lived here very long, so we're still trying each other on to see what fits. One friend in particular comes to mind. She's about my age and lives within walking distance of my home. She makes wonderful lavender cookies. Before coming to Africa, I didn't know that lavender was even edible. The cookies she makes remind me of shortbread laced with fragrant, purple bits of blossom. I've been privileged on several occasions to share times of prayer with her. She prays in Afrikaans, her primary language, and I pray in English. Even if we don't understand what the other is saying entirely, we've glimpsed enough of each other's lives to come together before heaven.

The other day, I decided to pay my friend a visit. When I arrived at her home, I was told, "she went to visit a friend." On my way home, we ran into each other! While I was looking for her at her home, she was looking for me at my home.

I like what C.S. Lewis said about friendship, "The next best thing to being wise oneself is to live in a circle of those who are." It's important that we surround ourselves with wise women who sharpen us spiritually.

week 33 reflections

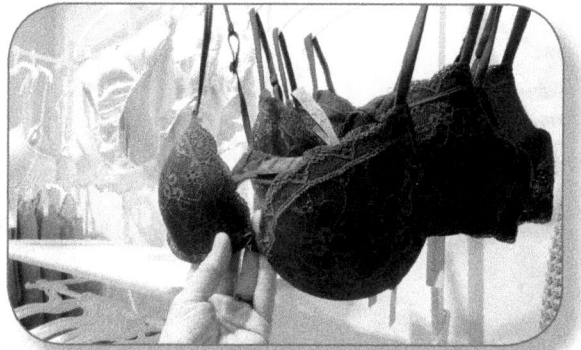

1. *"The next best thing to being wise oneself is to live in a circle of those who are."* What is your reaction to C. S. Lewis' quote? Do you agree with it?

2. God created man and woman in order to have a relationship with them. Relationships are central to the theme of God's Word. What relationships in your life are the best or strongest?

3. *"Friends are like bras. You need to try them on in order to find the perfect fit."* Think about your *"best friend."* What attributes does she have that you especially like?

4. *"Iron sharpens iron."* What does this mean to you? Why is this mentioned in the Bible?

34 Discernment versus Judgment

Several years ago, I preached a message on the difference between discernment and judgment. I remember looking in a thesaurus and being surprised that discernment and judgment were considered synonyms. From a biblical perspective the words have very different meanings.

The Bible says that God's people are to grow in discernment. Christians should grow in their understanding and insight of spiritual and natural matters. We are called to be both sharp and sensitive to situations and people around us. We should be able to discriminate between what is truth and falsehood. We should have farsightedness – the ability to examine an event and see its far-reaching effects. In the midst of discerning, there should also be an element of prayer. Those prayers should be filled with hope and the belief that the LORD is able to work in the midst of troubling times and among struggling people.

Judgment on the other hand means to render a verdict. In the original Greek context of the New Testament, the word judgment was used to describe eternal outcomes.

Romans 14:4 (HCSV) states, *"Who are you to criticize another's household slave? Before his own Lord he stands or falls. And he will stand. For the Lord is able to make him stand."* That same verse reminds us that each person stands or falls before his master. We do not have the right to judge or render an eternal outcome. Romans 2:1 (WEB) says, *"Therefore you are without excuse, O man, whoever you are who judge. For in that which you judge another, you condemn yourself. For you who judge practice the same things."* On a number of occasions, I have lived this verse. I've condemned and made judgments only to find myself practicing the same things that I've judged someone else for doing.

When I'm stressed, overworked, tired, or neglecting my personal walk of faith, the attitude of judgment seems to slip in. At first it goes unnoticed, and then circumstances often bring me face-to-face with my own weaknesses in areas where I've judged others. I thank the LORD for helping us to discern.

Ask Him to give you His eyes and ears of understanding.

May our words, and the attitudes of our hearts, be bathed in prayer. I want to be quick to remember the difference between discernment and judgment.

week 34 reflections

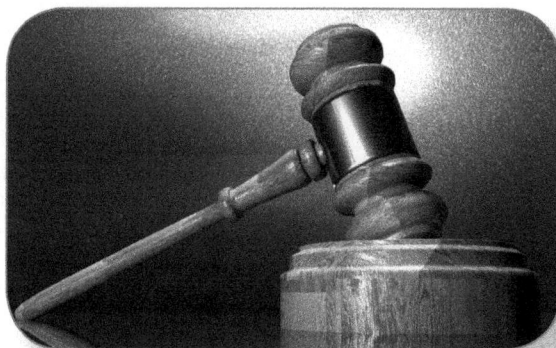

1. "We should be able to discriminate between what is truth and falsehood." This is indeed an ongoing struggle. We need to discern facts from opinions, as well. Think about a significant issue that is in the news right now. How can you be sure what is factual as you hear reports about this topic?

2. We judge others and we judge situations – every day! How can you be more sensitive to the needs and feelings of people around you and the circumstances you find yourself in at work or at home?

3. How can prayer help us to become more discerning and less judgmental?

4. *"You, then, why do you judge your brother or sister? Or why do you treat them with contempt? For we will all stand before God's judgment seat."* Romans 14:10 (NIV) This is a sobering thought. Only God has the right to judge. Think of a time when you realized you were judging someone. Write a short specific prayer asking God to forgive you.

35 *Landmarks*

Chris and I have been attending church on Sunday mornings in one of the townships not far from our home. The houses in the area are mostly tin shacks, and some are without electricity and running water. The roads are primarily dirt. There are several small stores. The stores sell bread and live chickens, others provide open-air haircuts. I enjoy seeing newly washed clothes hanging on lines, blowing in the breeze. I also like that the children in the community recognize our car and smile and wave. It helps, of course, that we often give them "sweeties."

Recently Chris had another ministry obligation, and I traveled to church on my own. Driving in South Africa is always interesting. That particular morning, there were baboons on the road, a duiker (a small African antelope) standing on a rock viewing its surroundings, donkeys and cattle grazing and crossing the road mindless of cars, and a small brush fire in a field.

Since there are no street signs in the township, I use a red flowering bush as a landmark to recognize where I turn to get to church. It occurred to me that morning that using a landmark that changed with the seasons was not the best plan.

Proverbs 22:28 (ESV) says, *"Do not move the ancient landmark that your fathers have set."* There are spiritual landmarks that God has put in place that should never be moved. Those landmarks do not change with the seasons. They are permanent and can always be relied on to guide our path. Job 24:2-8 discusses the consequences of landmarks being removed: orphans go without, widows struggle, the poor grow hungry, people lack basic necessities, and children suffer.

Jesus does not change with the seasons. He is the same yesterday, today, and forever. Jesus is the Light of World. He guides our path and keeps us from falling. He is the perfect landmark.

May the blessings of the LORD rest upon us. May we have a greater understanding of the perfect landmark sent by God.

week 35 reflections

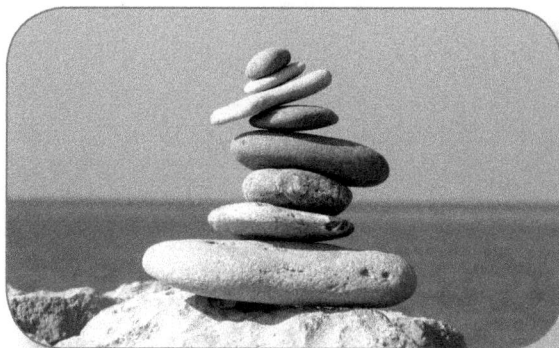

1. As you travel to work, church, school, or other familiar locations, you use landmarks to help you find the way. In addition to road signs, landmarks are often familiar buildings, natural formations, parks, trees, or other recognizable visual aids. Describe a short trip you take regularly using landmarks to guide the way rather than the names of streets.

2. Why did God want His people to use spiritual landmarks in the stories of the Old Testament?

3. Read Joshua 4:1-9. What is the purpose of the twelve stones?

4. Expand the thought: "Jesus is the perfect landmark."

36 *No Room at the Inn*

A number of years ago, I heard a pastor share a message on the chambers in our heart. He equated our heart to an inn with various rooms. I was challenged by his message to examine what resided in my heart. The rooms in my heart are filled with good things and at times not so good things. Things like pride, judgment, selfishness, and similar characteristics sometimes take up residence. My chambers are also filled with a love for ministry and service for family and friends.

Ministry and service are wonderful things. Helping and leading others to Christ should certainly be the focus of who we are and what we do. However, if the work of the LORD leaves no room for a thriving, growing relationship with the LORD of the Work, we're in trouble.

When Joseph and Mary arrived in Bethlehem, they looked for a room or chamber where they could rest. Mary's time had come to give birth to Jesus. They laid the Christ Child in a manger, an animal feeding trough, because there was no room for them in the inn. *"And she brought forth her firstborn son… and laid him in a manger, because there was no room for them in the inn."* Luke 2:7 (ASV)

These days I'm feeling like there are no vacancies available in my heart. Everything is full to the point of overflowing. I've been asking myself if I've made room for the Christ Child - room to learn and grow in my faith, room to spend quality and quantity time with the Savior, room to hear His voice and know I'm being directed by His Spirit.

One of my favorite passages of Scripture in the Old Testament is the story of Gideon. The Bible says that an angel of the LORD, or perhaps the LORD Himself, was sitting under a tree waiting for Gideon to take notice of Him. The LORD was waiting for Gideon to invite Him into the dwelling of his heart.

As women of faith, let's be purposeful to make room in our hearts for a thriving relationship with Jesus.

week 36 reflections

1. Sometimes our "doing" pushes out room in our heart for resting in the LORD's presence. Consider your schedule over the past week. What activities or events consumed your days? Did you take time to just "be" with the LORD? What are your thoughts about this issue of "being" with the LORD?

2. Read Luke 2, the story of the birth of Jesus. What particular aspects of this story stood out as you reread this familiar chapter?

3. Judges 6:13 (NIV) states: *"Pardon me, my LORD," Gideon replied, "but if the LORD is with us, why has all this happened to us?"* Have you thought the same thought and questioned where God is in times of trouble? How have you resolved this? Or if you haven't, describe your feelings about this issue.

4. Now read all of Judges 6. What promises or assurances of God do you recognize?

37 Creating a Team and a Dream

I was privileged recently to work with a wonderful ministry team. The gals were focused on preparing for their annual fundraiser. I was in awe of their creativity. Their efforts to raise money included not only a unique venue, but provided an amazing opportunity to share the Gospel. I was also impressed by how the ladies worked together as a unit. They seemed to know each other's strengths. They operated in cohesiveness and harmony. They also had a sense of community that made their time together fun.

Soon after my time with the "dream team," my husband and I hosted our annual ministry board meeting. We generally travel to the U.S. once a year, so our face-to-face time with those who govern our ministry is limited. This group of important people, however, is faithful to keep in touch via e-mail and Facebook. They are also faithful to pray and encourage us. They are invaluable to us not only in ministry but on a personal level. At the meeting, one of the members shared an excerpt from a book on team building by Max Lucado. Listed below are some key points from the information he shared:

Teamwork is vital both in personal life and in ministry. The efforts of a team achieve more for the Kingdom of God than we can accomplish individually. Teamwork enhances our lives and the lives of those we work with. I love the saying, "It takes a team to create a dream."

• Commitment that inspires results	• Creativity that enlarges the team's potential
• Contributions that make a difference	• Conflict management to reduce tension rapidly
• Competency that raises a standard	
• Communication for effectiveness	• Cohesiveness that allows change to be rapid
• Cooperation that creates harmony	• Community that makes the journey fun
• Chemistry that enhances personal connection	

May we always remember that a team can achieve more for the Kingdom of God then we can accomplish individually.

week 37 reflections

1. The Bible mentions "the body" – the community that relies on the gifts and passions of each individual to work together for the good of the Kingdom of God. Read 1 Corinthians 12 and list three statements in this chapter that are particularly significant to you.

2. 1 Corinthians 12:27 (NIV) states *"Now you are the body of Christ, and each one of you is a part of it."* What part do you play in "the body of Christ"? (Spend time thinking and praying about this before you write your answer. You may play a larger part than you think you do.)

3. Read through the list of components listed in the devotional that help create a team. Which one specifically "jumps out at you"? Why?

4. *"It takes a team to create a dream."* Think about a time in your life that this was especially true and summarize that scenario.

38 *A Big Fat Lip*

I'm sure there are wonderful dentists in Mokopane. In fact, I met one at a dinner party. But somehow my confidence wanes when medical clinics are located right next to witch doctor establishments. So, when I lost a crown last fall, I waited until I returned to the U.S. to have the permanent crown put back in place.

When I arrived in the Midwest to see family, I made a dental appointment with my mom's dentist. The process of replacing my crown took several visits. During one such visit, while the dental assistant was attempting to remove the temporary crown, she slipped and hit my lip with a piece of equipment. My lip broke open like I had been in a high school girl fight (although there was no hair pulling), and it swelled to the point that it was uncomfortable. The assistant was extremely apologetic. In fact, she offered to excuse herself, but I asked her to continue to help me. Accidents happen. There have been times in ministry where mistakes have taken place. Mistakes happen because we are practicing at life. Sometimes I've been the recipient of someone else's mistake, and sometimes someone else has been the recipient of my error. I think it is wrong to allow someone to excuse themselves from our lives because he or she has hurt us. I'm not talking about an abuser, or someone who lacks the maturity to maintain a healthy relationship; rather, I'm thinking of when a momentary lapse in judgment occurs between friends or ministry partners.

I appreciate those who have given me a second chance. When Chris and I first moved to the Eastern Plains of Colorado, I was invited by the pastor of our new church to share an announcement about an upcoming ladies' event. I was late to church and neglected my responsibility. The pastor didn't write me off. In fact, over the next few years, I was asked to share from the pulpit on numerous occasions.

Several years ago, a friend distorted some information about me. I made the decision to talk with her and today our relationship is stronger than ever.

We need to be women of second chances. May we allow others to make mistakes as we also surround ourselves with friends and ministry associates who allow us to err in judgment and grow spiritually.

week 38 reflections

1. "Second chances" are really about offering forgiveness multiple times if needed. Read Psalm 130:3-5 (NIV). *"If you, LORD, kept a record of sins, LORD, who could stand? But with you there is forgiveness, so that we can, with reverence, serve you. I wait for the LORD, my whole being waits, and in his word I put my hope."* Summarize these verses in "today's language."

2. Think about a time in your life when you needed a "second chance." Did you get it? Or are you still wishing you had been forgiven and been allowed to try again? Write about that time and your reactions to it.

3. Forgiveness takes intentionality to love and reconcile, and the heart of God to direct our thoughts and actions. Is there someone in your family who needs a "second chance"? What can you do?

4. How can you become more willing to forgive – and grow in love intentionally?

39 *Lost and Found*

There's a story in Luke 15 about a woman who lost a coin. She had ten silver coins and somehow misplaced one. The Bible says that she lit a lamp, swept her home, and searched carefully until she found the missing treasure. When the coin was found she called her neighbors together to celebrate. She wanted her friends to rejoice with her that what was once lost had now been found.

Our small goat herd in South Africa recently disappeared. Gerhard, the shepherd, had taken the goats to a neighbor's property for weed control. One evening they were simply gone. Gerhard's first thought was that the goats had been stolen. Livestock are considered a precious commodity here. Gerhard searched for several days. He wasn't able to find a break in the fence line or even tracks to follow.

On Saturday nights, Chris and I host a small community church in our home. As a church family, we prayed and asked the LORD to bring the herd home. A couple days later a local farm worker spotted the goats some distance away in a lush meadow next to a dam.

What treasures have we lost: friendship, finances, peace of mind, joy in serving others, a relationship with a family member, ministry opportunities? The search for lost treasure can be laborious, intense, emotionally draining, and time consuming. Sometimes there's no breach in the fence to give us a clue or footprints to follow in the soil.

The woman in Scripture lit a lamp and looked hard into the night. I think those same principles apply in our lives. The Word of God is a guiding light. We can't expect the things that are dear to us to always come easily, and we can't be afraid or ashamed to ask for help in our quest.

I've lost a spiritual gift that was once an important part of my life. I'm not sure how it was lost, or where it went. Like my friend, Gerhard, there doesn't seem to be guiding markers indicating where I can find it. I just know it's a treasure, and that there is a lesson for me in searching and reclaiming something I value. I'm spending time in prayer and Bible study asking the LORD for guidance. I won't give up too quickly.

Let's understand that recovery takes effort on our part. We need to be honest with someone we trust, ask for help, and celebrate together when we find our treasure.

week 39 reflections

1. We often spend time searching for lost items: keys, glasses, homework, a file on our computer. The woman in "the parable of the lost coin" doesn't give up. What can you learn from this parable?

2. Think about someone or something that is or was considered a treasure in your life that is now gone. *"The search for lost treasure can be laborious, intense, emotionally draining, and time consuming."* Is there anything you can do to recover your lost treasure?

3. In Luke 15:1-7, Jesus tells the "parable of the lost sheep." Read through this story and summarize it. What principle is Jesus sharing?

4. List three important steps mentioned in this line: *"We need to be honest with someone we trust, ask for help, and celebrate together when we find our treasure."* Are there other steps you can think of?

40 *Rookie*

Every rookie preacher should be open to tips that might help him or her be more successful in ministering to the church family. We may not preach from a pulpit every Sunday, but we certainly have a pulpit - it just looks different. Our pulpit might be a living room where we host community Bible studies. It might be a table at a favorite restaurant where we frequently meet and encourage others. We also may not have a congregation that gathers each week, but we have a congregation – again, it just looks different. We each have those whom the LORD has entrusted into our care to lead, teach, and guide.

Listed below are my ten tips:

1. **Get to know God.** Never settle for knowing about God. Make it your life's greatest ambition to really know and love the God who loves you.

2. **Be a Bible person, not an issue person.** It is tempting to let certain issues define your ministry, but platforms and issues will shift. Place biblical truth over an issue.

3. **Determine never to be a glory thief.** Decide now that showing off has no place in your life. Always point others to Christ and not to yourself.

4. **Learn to discriminate feedback.** Learn to evaluate and discern feedback, both positive and negative. It's important to recognize hyped-up praise and nasty criticism.

5. **Don't let skill get ahead of biblical awareness and God consciousness.** People will praise someone in the public eye. They will also praise someone with natural talent and ability. It is important to be biblically sound.

6. **Don't let your ministry profile get ahead of your character.** Let your ministry move forward at God's pace; otherwise, duties may get too heavy for your character to bear.

7. **Be proactive, not self-promoting.** It's important to ask God for ministry opportunities, but be wary of leaving God behind as you seek after ministry.

8. **Learn to read wisely.** Chose quality reading materials over quantity. It is also important to expand beyond favorite authors and topics.

9. **Don't journey alone.** For you to be healthy it is necessary to have peer relationships and mentor relationships.

10. **Have a lifelong conversation with God.** Your personal walk with the LORD should be first and foremost in every aspect of your life.

week 40 reflections

1. *"We may not preach from a pulpit every Sunday, but we certainly have a pulpit - it just looks different."* Where is your pulpit? Explain how you might impact the lives of those around you.

2. Number 2 in the list of tips states: *"Be a Bible person, not an issue person."* What issues have you been wrestling with? What steps can you take to become more of a Bible person, and less of an issue person?

3. A wise person once said, *"You can get a lot done if you don't care who gets the credit."* Item 7 states: "Be proactive, not self-promoting." What do you think this means?

4. Reread the list of "10 Tips Every Rookie Preacher Should Hear." How does it pertain to your own calling and scope of responsibilities?

41 *Hard Questions*

On Thursday afternoons, I teach a ladies' Bible study in one of the local villages. Five to seven ladies attend on any given week. Yesterday, the ladies wanted something different. They wanted to have a "q and a" session – which is not my favorite forum (especially since I would be the one answering the questions).

The first question was a doozy, "Where in the Bible does it talk about female circumcision?" I took a deep breath and explained that God doesn't want women to be circumcised. I also included the biblical truth that God created women to enjoy sexual intimacy within marriage. One of the ladies talked for a few minutes in Sotho. I didn't understand what she was saying with my ears but understood what she was saying with my heart. She was relating her personal story of mutilation. When I asked the translator specifically what was being said, she replied, "Our friend doesn't like it and wants it to be different."

I learned from the ladies that it is still part of some tribal cultures for women to be circumcised. Young girls are taken into the bush and "surgery" is performed by a local witch doctor. The ladies wanted to know what could be done to protect their daughters and granddaughters. I encouraged them to pray, to talk with their husbands and tribal leaders, to take a stand for the truth of God's Word, and to be creative. I also encouraged the ladies to be thankful for the changes regarding this issue that are already taking place: open discussion, education, and understanding that God has a better plan.

Anne Frank asked, *"Why do some people have to starve, while there are surpluses rotting in other parts of the world? And why are people so crazy?"* There are no easy answers to some questions. There are no quick fixes or simple explanations to some of the puzzles of life. I can't change tribal beliefs that have existed for generations, but I can pray and use my voice to speak truth. I am also asking the LORD for divine opportunities to discuss the situation with the local pastors, tribal chiefs, and leaders.

As Christian women, what can we do about the troubling matters of life? First, I think we can listen with our hearts to those who are hurting. I also think we can pray and speak the truth of God's Word. We can't be silent when others are being abused. We can also use our sphere of influence to motivate others into action, and finally we can remain thankful for the changes we see taking place. May we be creative instruments of change.

week 41 reflections

1. How do you know that God loves, respects, and honors women? Write down the Scriptures that give you this assurance.

2. What cultural, religious, or governmental issues did Jesus deal with? Think of a specific instance where Jesus refuted the law or societal norms of the day.

3. What issues in today's culture seem to be troubling and insurmountable?

4. The devotional gives us some specific ways to deal with issues that seem to be beyond fixing. We can:
   - listen with our hearts to those who are hurting
   - pray and speak the truth of God's Word
   - use our sphere of influence to motivate others into action

   What other strategies can we use to change cultural norms that go against God's Law?

42 Wise and Foolish

The wise woman actively builds her house. *"Wisdom has built her house; she has set up its seven pillars. She has prepared her meat and mixed her wine; she has also set her table. She has sent out her servants, and she calls from the highest point of the city, 'Let all who are simple come to my house!' To those who have no sense she says, 'Come, eat my food and drink the wine I have mixed. Leave your simple ways and you will live; walk in the way of insight.'"* Proverbs 9:1-6 (NIV)

The wise woman doesn't take the building and maintenance process of her life lightly. She establishes pillars in her personal development, foundational standards that she is unwilling to compromise. Some versions of the Bible say, "She even kills beasts." Perhaps she's a dragon slayer of sorts, who refuses to allow any "beastly" thing to control her life. More than likely, the beasts are the protein portion of the meals she prepares, but I like the image of her fighting and overcoming wild things that would try to harm her and those she serves. She mixes her wine. She understands there is no divine wisdom without the Holy Spirit's activity in her life. She sets her table waiting for others to come and dine.

She is energized about the things of God and faithfully prepares herself to serve and care for others. The Bible also tells us that she has partners in ministry - maidens who help her spread the Good News. She's not afraid to proclaim Christ openly. In fact, "She calls out from the highest point in the city." She invites everyone to come learn about the LORD: the simple, the wise, the rich, and the poor. She doesn't compromise spiritual principles and explains to all who will listen the importance of repentance and living rightly.

There are so many things that we can glean from Proverbs 9. Each time I read this passage, I learn something new. Lately what spoke to me specifically about the wise woman was her preparedness. Being prepared for the unexpected has an entirely new meaning in South Africa. The Bible tells us to be ready in season and out of season.

Jesus cursed the fig tree because it was fully leafed and looked like it should bear good fruit, but it only looked good - there was no substance. I don't want to just look good; I want there to be substance in my life. In order to have good fruit, I must prepare myself spiritually.

May we seek the LORD to become wise and creative women, who are prepared at all times to serve and care for others.

week 42 reflections

1. Read Proverbs 9. Make a list of the attributes of this wise woman.

2. Sometimes this "wise woman" seems too unattainable in today's world. Think about and list the kinds of virtues or abilities today's woman might demonstrate.

3. Being prepared is an ongoing challenge. It is more than having extra food in the freezer. What can you do to "be prepared"?

4. Read Mark 14:1-9 which briefly tells the story of the woman with the alabaster jar of perfume. What was this woman's motivation?

43 *Hold Onto Your Bosom*

Chris and I live in the bush. To get to our home a four-wheel drive vehicle is required. The road is rough, rutted, and extremely sandy. The other day as Chris and I were traveling, Chris muttered just as he hit a large rock, "Hold onto your bosom."

Several days after Chris' comment, I was visiting with a woman in one of the local townships who speaks Sotho. Conversing was limited. The woman was sitting under a tree washing dishes, and I was sitting on a log next to her. The elderly lady touched her partially exposed breasts and then pointed toward mine. It's not uncommon to see mammaries in South Africa, even at church. I'm not sure what my friend was saying. She might have been asking if I have children, telling me that she needs a bra, asking my size, or even indicating that she needed food for her orphaned grandchildren. When I didn't respond, she talked louder and, like my car ride, held onto her bosom.

Sometimes we just need to hold on. Life can get bumpy, and the ride can get tiresome. Life can also be thrilling, so thrilling that we shake our bodies with laughter and need to hold onto "the girls."

In Colorado, the road home would sometimes be rough and rutted also. We never know what we will see because of a rut, or from the top of the hill, or what lies just beyond the bend. I was teaching a class of second and third grade gifted readers a number of years ago when during group reading time one of the students read aloud the word "bosom." He then proceeded to explain to the others what the word meant. It was very titillating for the children and caused me to laugh out loud.

Over and over again in Scripture, we see rocky and rough life paths producing miraculous and thrilling adventures.

We serve a great God. He is with us on the rough roads and the thrilling rides, so get ready to hold onto your bosoms.

week 43 reflections

1. Life can indeed "get bumpy." Summarize a time in your life that was especially "bumpy."

2. Some of the women mentioned in the Bible are Ruth, Esther, the widow at Zarephath, and Mary, the mother of Jesus. Select one of these women, locate and read the story about her situation in Scripture, and then summarize her need to "hold onto her bosom."

3. Read the story of Sarah, Abraham's wife, in Genesis 17:1-19. Explain how this story fits with the comment: *"Over and over again in Scripture, we see rocky and rough life paths producing miraculous and thrilling adventures."*

4. Why do you think God chooses "rocky and rough life paths" for us? Explain your thinking.

44 *The Belt of Truth*

I was a young girl in Sunday school when I first learned about the Armor of God. The Apostle Paul mentions the Belt of Truth in the Book of Ephesians. During biblical times, a belt was the most important piece of a soldier's armor. The belt held the scabbard where the sword was placed. Some historians believe that the belt, in order to protect the vital organs, was several inches wide.

The television show "Myth Busters" recently did a reenactment about a deputy sheriff who was shot by an assailant. The bullet was deflected by the deputy's belt. There was no harm to the officer. Ephesians 5 tells us to be strong in the LORD and in the power of His might. We are to arm ourselves with the things of God so we can stand against evil. Part of arming ourselves includes putting on the Belt of Truth. Truth should cleave to us like a belt cleaves to our body. We are sanctified by God's truth, and the truth is His Word. (John 17:17) Sanctified has several meanings. In this passage, one of those meanings includes being set apart from danger, protected from evil, and kept safe by God.

Close to where I live, there are a number of villages in which I've noticed children with strings tied around their waists. Because the people who live in rural South African townships are generally very poor, I assumed that the children were wearing worn clothing.

I have since learned that a string is placed around a baby's waist by a local witch doctor when he or she dedicates a baby. These belts are believed to protect the child. There is a sizeable fee associated with the yearly replacement of the string, yet every year the family pays the witch doctor to replace it. The fee is paid in the form of money, animals, or food. People are deceived spiritually and fleeced financially. Evil abounds in our world.

God freely gives us truth and protection. The Belt of Truth is ours. Truth will set you free. (John 8:32) We simply need to place it about our waist and buckle it tightly. The purchase price was paid by Jesus at Calvary. This belt also does not need to be replaced every year. The Word of God is ageless. It doesn't change. It never needs to be replaced.

As Christian women, we must arm ourselves daily with the Belt of Truth remembering that we are strong in the Lord and in the power of His might.

week 44 reflections

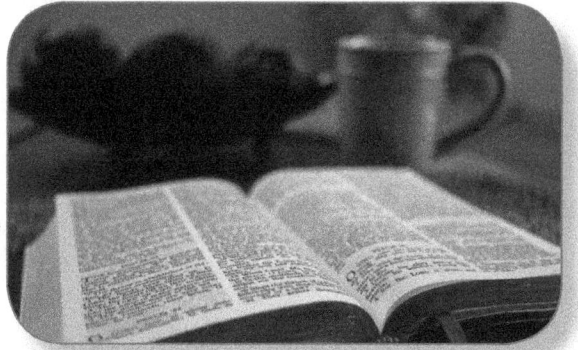

1. Read Ephesians 6:10-20. List the components of the Armor of God and their meanings.

2. How does this reference to the "full armor of God" sustain you in difficult times?

3. In Ephesians 6 (NIV), we read: *"For our struggle is not against flesh and blood, but against the rulers, against the authorities, against the powers of this dark world, and against the spiritual forces of evil in the heavenly realms."* What does this mean?

4. The world is filled with deception and counterfeit beliefs. The witch doctor in the town mentioned in the devotional intentionally deceived the people in the village. By what means are we deceived in our culture? How can we be sure of the Truth?

45 Nothing Too Deep, Too Dark, Too Dirty

Chris and I recently hired a local plumbing company. On a Monday, about mid-morning, the workers arrived in a small truck. The sign on the side of their green truck read, "There's nothing too deep, too dark, or too dirty."

In the Book of Acts, Paul received a vision about a man from Macedonia pleading for help. He and Silas then traveled to Philippi. Along a stream, just outside the city, they met Lydia, who believed the teachings of Paul and was immediately baptized. Paul and Silas also brought deliverance to a demon-possessed slave girl nearby.

Although the apostle and his assistant were following the leading of the Holy Spirit, they ended up in a very deep, very dark, and very dirty place. They were arrested illegally, publicly stripped of their clothing, tied to a post, beaten with wooden clubs, and placed in the inner dungeon of a prison. The Bible says *"about midnight, Paul and Silas were praying and singing hymns to God... Suddenly there was such a violent earthquake that the foundations of the prison were shaken. At once all the prison doors flew open, and everyone's chains came loose."* Acts 16:25-26 (NIV)

In this story, the man in Paul's vision represented the people of Macedonia. Paul and Silas' spiritual encounters in the region were powerful and prolific. The city officials wanted Paul and Silas to leave Philippi in secret. The two respectfully refused. The Gospel was never meant to be kept secret but to be shared by a stream, in the city square, among those in prisons, and in homes and churches.

Ministry begins with a vision or a call to assist those who are "pleading for help." Along the way our encounters will be powerful and prolific. We may also find ourselves in deep, dark, and dirty places. May our voices in those difficult places be filled with worship and praise to our God and in the midst of those praises may others find Jesus.

week 45 reflections

1. Read Acts 16:6-40. What did you find particularly meaningful in this story?

2. Paul and Silas were following the lead of the Holy Spirit. Why would the Holy Spirit lead them into a place where *"they were arrested illegally, publicly stripped of their clothing, tied to a post, beaten with wooden clubs, and placed in the inner dungeon of a prison"*?

3. The travels of Paul and Silas - and of all Jesus' disciples - were difficult and life-threatening. What caused them to continue to share God's Truth?

4. *"Ministry begins with a vision or a call to assist those who are 'pleading for help.'"* What outreach or ministry have you been involved in that started with a vision or a call? Why are you involved?

46 *The Fly and Axe*

Porcia joined our ministry staff quite some time ago. She is a dear friend, ministry partner, cultural advisor, and translator. She wears many hats and fills big shoes.

Right after she joined our ministry team, Porcia confided in me that she had been in a long-term relationship with a man that recently ended. They had known each other for four years. The man professed to be a Christian. He had proposed, and arrangements were being made for him to meet her family. He convinced Porcia that since they were engaged, sexual intimacy was okay. When Porica didn't hear from him for several days, she became worried and called his cell phone. The man's wife answered the phone. Porica had been lied to, tricked, and manipulated. When Porcia learned that she was pregnant, she immediately left her local church. She was concerned about public humiliation.

Porcia assumed that when she told Chris and me about the baby that we would fire her and remove her from our lives. Instead, Chris and I told her that we viewed her as a spiritual daughter and would not abandon her.

A Chinese proverb says, *"Don't remove a fly from your friend's forehead with an axe."* In other words, if your friend has a blemish or a problem, don't try to help by using a large, sharp instrument. As Christian women, there will be times when our friends, peers in ministry, spiritual daughters, or natural daughters are deceived to sin. If we try to help them by using an axe, we'll hurt them in a way that causes long-term emotional and spiritual damage. Galatians 6:1 says that if a person is caught doing something wrong, those who are spiritual should restore the person gently.

Porcia recognized that she had been deceived. She knew it was wrong to have sex outside of marriage. She was struggling with her own guilt and shame. She understood that God had forgiven her but was having trouble forgiving herself. She didn't need me to preach at her; she didn't need me to point out the error of her ways. She needed gentleness and restoration. She needed to know that Chris and I loved her and that we would love her baby.

We must search for God's wise answers in His Word, and apply them generously. The Bible is our source for truth regarding deception, sin, repentance, restoration, and love.

week 46 reflections

1. Candor is often the kindest and most honorable way to express yourself and help others avoid the perils of false flattery or mistaken confidence. What are your thoughts about this Chinese proverb: *"Don't remove a fly from your friend's forehead with an axe"*?

2. We've all sinned. Sometimes we are deceived, and sometimes we simply make wrong choices. What lesson have you learned from a situation in your life where you neglected to follow God's laws and that decision resulted in a bad outcome?

3. Galatians 6:1 (NIV) states: *"Brothers and sisters, if someone is caught in a sin, you who live by the Spirit should restore that person gently. But watch yourselves, or you also may be tempted."* Rewrite this in more contemporary words.

4. *"The Bible is our source for truth regarding deception, sin, repentance, restoration, and love."* 2 Timothy 3:16-17 (NIV) states: *"All Scripture is God-breathed and is useful for teaching, rebuking, correcting, and training in righteousness, so that the servant of God may be thoroughly equipped for every good work."* How do these two statements impact your life?

47 Not All Feedback is Created Equal

I recently read an online article, by a pastor, on the subject of feedback. The article began with the words, "Not all feedback is created equal." I agree. I think it is important that we hear feedback and learn to give it. I also think it is important to evaluate feedback, especially in times of static. The appropriate response to feedback is to listen and then prayerfully consider what has been shared. Sometimes it takes time to process, to understand what has been spoken, and to evaluate the intent and reality of it.

The Bible tells us that David was a man after God's heart. He was able to sift through the feedback received. He ignored the criticism of his brothers, yet humbly responded to the challenges of the Prophet Nathan. Once, when David had fled the city of Jerusalem because of Absalom's rebellion, numbers of people abandoned him. His trusted servant Shimei, pelted him with rocks and cursed, *"Get out of here, you murderer, you scoundrel!"* 2 Samuel 16:7 (NLT) King David, was stunned and wondered whether God had instigated the feedback, so he did not lash out. He didn't want to harm someone out of anger or personal retribution, so he deferred his right to punish.

As Christian women, we need close friends and ministry associates in our lives who will give us proper feedback. I have several friends with the gift of encouragement. In almost every situation, their feedback is very positive. While I appreciate loyal words, their feedback may not be supported by reality. A number of people in my life process situations by using criticism - for some it's a personality trait. For others, their spiritual giftedness involves a direct approach. Hoorahs and humdrums offer opposite ends of the spectrum.

We need truth-tellers who offer prayer-based, scriptural, discerning feedback. Feedback should not be based on a person's mood. We need to seek out feedback with specific examples, because generalizations can be easily misunderstood. Even if the feedback is challenging, the presentation should inspire hope and appreciation for the efforts and hard work exemplified. While everyone misses the mark from time to time, feedback should acknowledge the service and time given.

May the LORD help us to welcome feedback in our lives and ministries, and may He also remind us that not all feedback is created equal.

week 47 reflections

1. Share an incident in your life where feedback was given that either encouraged you or bothered you.

2. *"The Bible tells us that David was a man after God's heart. He was able to sift through the feedback he received in his life. He ignored the criticism of his brothers, yet responded to the challenges of the Prophet Nathan."* Read 2 Samuel 12. Summarize the role Nathan played in this story.

3. 1 Thessalonians 5:11-12 (BSB) states: *"Therefore encourage and build one another up, just as you are already doing. But we ask you, brothers, to acknowledge those who work diligently among you, who preside over you in the Lord and give you instruction."* How does encouragement keep you focused?

4. Who in your life needs feedback right now… either encouragement or some "prayer-based, Scripture-founded, discerning feedback"? How can you be involved in a supportive way?

48 *Hooray for the Red, White, and Blue*

Chris and I generally spend three months of the year in the U.S. We arrive in December to celebrate the holidays with family, and then travel to Denver to meet with board members, to host ministry events, to complete year-end accounting, and to enjoy time with friends.

I love our life in South Africa. People in South Africa are very curious about America and her citizens. Our translator uses Tyler Perry movies as a guide to what American life is like. Another friend, who enjoys reading Louis L'Amour novels, thinks that most U.S. residents wear cowboy hats, ride horses, and raise cattle. South Africans are especially curious about American politics and policies. Many Americans are likewise curious about South Africans and others who live in distant places. Recently someone asked me if it was true that people in other parts of the world dislike Americans. I'm not familiar with most parts of the world, but I can honestly say in my limited travels that I have found just the opposite to be true.

We're not a perfect nation. We have undeniable problems, but as women who lead others, I believe it's important that we model humility, prayer, and respect for our country and her leaders, rather than curses and denouncements. When asked, I am happy to share my opinions. I try to preface my ideas with the serious responsibility I've been given by God to pray for my nation.

1 Timothy 2:1-2 (NIV) says, *"I urge, then, first of all that petitions, prayers, intercession and thanksgiving be made for all people – for kings and all those in authority, that we may live peaceful and quiet lives in all godliness and holiness."* We are commanded by God to petition (asking with factual detail and mentioning His supreme power to answer like people do in a court of law), to pray (talk to the LORD about everything and listen in return), to intercede (stand in a breech and believe the LORD for victory), and to be thankful (have a good and godly attitude). We are especially to remember those in authority (spiritual leaders, political leaders, and those who have social/cultural influence).

We need to have peaceful and quiet lives so we can focus on eternal matters, and discern the heart of our God, who wants everyone to have spiritual understanding and know Him as Savior.

week 48 reflections

1. *"Our translator uses Tyler Perry movies as a guide to what American life is like. Another friend, who enjoys reading Louis L'Amour novels, thinks that most U.S. residents wear cowboy hats, ride horses, and raise cattle."* It's interesting to hear about the stereotyped ideas that people in other countries have about Americans. What comes to mind when you picture the people of Africa?

2. Why would God want us to pray specifically for our leaders?

3. Do you think God has blessed the United States? If so, in what ways?

4. *"We are commanded by God to petition (asking with factual detail and mentioning His supreme power to answer like people do in a court of law), to pray (talk to the LORD about everything and listen in return), to intercede (stand in a breech and believe the LORD for victory), and to be thankful (have a good and godly attitude). We are especially to remember those in authority (spiritual leaders, political leaders, and those who have social/ cultural influence)."* These are important components of prayer. Write a prayer for our leaders using these guidelines.

49 Holding Onto What is Good

Lately, I've been studying the Book of First Thessalonians. Paul preached the Gospel in the synagogue at Thessalonica, and a number of Jews were converted to Christ. The apostle was accused of causing a civil disturbance and the accusations caused him to leave the city as a wise and ready response. The church was, at most, a few months old. There were no mature leaders in place to oversee the ministry. Paul made several attempts to return to the city, yet according to 1 Thessalonians 2:17-18, Satan disrupted his plans. Paul experienced great anxiety over the wellbeing of the church and sent Timothy to check on the welfare of the believers. Some types of stress and anxiety are warranted and prompted by the Holy Spirit. After Timothy returned, Paul penned his first letter to the Thessalonians. The content contains both words of encouragement and words of correction.

I am especially convicted by Paul's final verses which include the following instruction: *"Do not stifle the Holy Spirit. Do not scoff at prophecies, but test everything that is said. Hold on to what is good. Stay away from every kind of evil."* 1 Thessalonians 5:19-22 (NLT)

I was at a restaurant recently and felt impressed by the LORD to spiritually encourage another customer. I wanted to listen and be led by the Holy Spirit, but I was with a family member and was worried about what she would think. I compromised. I anonymously paid for the man's breakfast but did not speak a word to him. The waitress, who was serving my table, shared that the aged man ate breakfast at the restaurant each morning. He was the caregiver for his wife and would often take home a cinnamon roll to her. The word of encouragement that I had been given included praise for his service to others. The LORD wanted me to express to him that He saw his struggles and understood his weariness.

The Holy Spirit is present in our lives. Believers should hold on to what is good and not stifle His promptings. We shouldn't scoff, belittle, or make fun of prophetic gifts.

God wants to use us. We must listen to the Holy Spirit and not stifle His gifts. I am sure that the elderly man in the restaurant was blessed to have the cost of his breakfast covered, yet I know that the LORD had more in store for him that morning. God wanted this special gentleman to hear a sweet word of encouragement, strength, and comfort.

week 49 reflections

1. *"According to 1 Thessalonians 2:17-18, Satan disrupted Paul's plans."* Why would Satan intervene?

2. Has there been a time when the Holy Spirit urged you to do something specific, talk to someone, or step in to help in a situation, but you declined to act? Summarize what went on in your spirit.

3. Think about these important words: *"Do not stifle the Holy Spirit, do not scoff at prophesies, test everything, cling to what is good, and stay away from evil."* What can you do to "test everything"?

4. Prophecy is sharing spiritual truth. Prophecy is something that seems out of our "comfort zone." Do you know someone personally or have you watched someone on TV who is a prophet? How do you feel about their insights? How can you know whether to believe what they say?

50 *Unteachable*

I heard a story recently about a father who gave instruction to his son on how to take care of a household chore. As the dad was talking, the son kept interrupting, "I know… I know, Dad." When the son had completed the task, the father went to check the boy's work. It was a disaster. Thankfully, the son was humble enough to admit, "I didn't know…."

The Great Commission found in Matthew 28:18-20 includes the words "teach" and "disciple." Teaching and being taught need to be a way of life for every believer.

A number of years ago, I was involved in an intercessory prayer group. As part of the weekly meetings, the group was studying a book on prayer. I found the book interesting, but I struggled with some of the concepts. The material discussed issues of prayer that were unfamiliar to me – things I'd never thought about or experienced. I was unteachable.

When I say "unteachable," I mean I felt I had it all figured out already. I believed I was right, and couldn't be persuaded even when Scripture was introduced to help me re-evaluate things. Sometime later, after I'd grown in my prayer life, I realized that the information in the book was invaluable. I learned I should always be learning.

Ministering to someone who is unteachable is extremely difficult. Recently, I encountered two such women. Both women were engaged in lifestyle sin but were justifying their actions. They both approached me for help but didn't like the biblical truth I shared with them. I wasn't harsh with the ladies. I was kind, compassionate, and loving, but, none-the-less, their hearts were unmovable.

Trying to help a person whose heart is set in stone or is sinking in the mire of sensual preferences, whose ears won't hear instruction, can be very frustrating. But, a person who is teachable and enjoys learning and testing new spiritual truths is a delight. Being unteachable is thinking I have all the answers. As Christians, we should always be learning. We have never truly arrived until we arrive in heaven. The Great Commission found in Matthew 28:18-20 includes the word "teach." Teaching and being taught need to be a way of life for every believer.

week 50 reflections

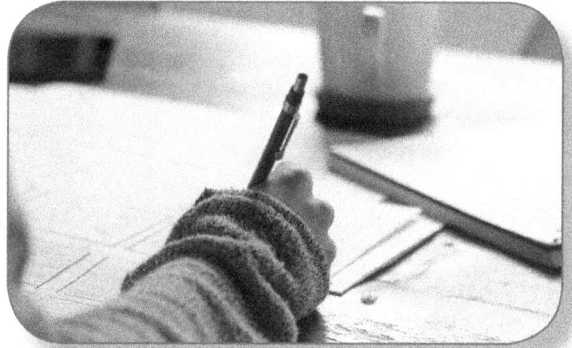

1. We all know people who appear to be "unteachable." No matter what you say, they have already determined their thoughts and actions. How can you best handle the situation when you confront someone who is "unteachable"?

2. Think about the story of Moses and Pharaoh in Egypt. Pharaoh responded to Moses: *"Who is the LORD, that I should obey him and let Israel go? I do not know the LORD and I will not let Israel go."* Exodus 5:2 (NIV) Why did God harden Pharaoh's heart and make him "unteachable"?

3. In Ezekiel 36:25-27 (NIV), the LORD states: *"I will sprinkle clean water on you, and you will be clean; I will cleanse you from all your impurities and from all your idols. I will give you a new heart and put a new spirit in you; I will remove from you your heart of stone and give you a heart of flesh. And I will put my Spirit in you and move you to follow my decrees and be careful to keep my laws."* It seems that a "heart of stone" would be the condition for an "unteachable" person. What are your thoughts about this verse?

4. *"We have never truly arrived until we arrive in heaven."* Perhaps you have never thought of this before. How can this become a "lifestyle" for you? List specific ways you can focus on this thought.

51 Recognize, Release, and Remember

A number of years ago, I was visiting a friend who was in charge of a rather large women's organization. I asked her what was being done within her organization to nurture women in their spiritual calling. Her response indicated that she didn't recognize women in her midst being called by God into ministry. My heart still grieves. Every woman is called to some form of ministry. There are also women participating in most organizations that have a specific ministry call. We are required by God to help and nurture others in pursuing the LORD's plan, to "equip" the body. Paul models this requirement in Scripture. We find him throughout the New Testament helping younger men to pursue God's calling.

Porcia has worked with me for quite some time. Early on I could tell that her time of ministry with our organization would be limited. I recognized that her giftedness went far beyond working as a translator. She's an amazing young woman. She can lead worship, teach Bible studies, preach a sermon, give godly counsel and wisdom, reach different people groups and ages… and the list could go on. Helping our ministry with translation is only a stepping stone for other things that God has in store for her.

Recently a new ministry opportunity opened for Porcia. She's debating about whether to walk in this new calling or to stay with Strong Cross Ministries. Porcia is nervous about her future. I can't choose her path, but I can pray and encourage her to seek God and His direction for her life. There's a selfish part of me that doesn't want to lose her. She's become a spiritual daughter to me. I enjoy spending time with her.

In my mind, she can't be replaced. Yet, I also know that she's not mine to keep. I understand the importance of releasing her to move on for her own development. Transition is hard for all involved. I know if I don't release her that eventually our relationship both personally and spiritually will be damaged. I also understand that if strife develops between us that those we serve will also be hurt.

We must be diligent in praying, pondering, and remembering with love.

week 51 reflections

1. Have you served in a church, an outreach, or a ministry where you didn't feel as if your gifts had been truly recognized? Summarize that situation and your feelings.

2. The list of spiritual gifts can be found in 1 Corinthians 12. Read that chapter and list the gifts mentioned. What other gifts can you think of that God can use?

3. Name a gift of the spirit that others have noticed in you. How has this been recognized and reinforced in your life?

4. When someone transitions in ministry, it is also important to be committed to remembering the person in a positive light. Often we get defensive, annoyed, or even bitter when someone moves on to another ministry. (Perhaps a pastor in your church has moved on and left the congregation with mixed feelings.) How can we remember the person in a positive light?

52 *Complete Surrender*

"All to Jesus I surrender. All to Him I freely give. I will ever love and trust Him. In His presence daily live. I surrender all. I surrender all. All to Thee, my blessed Savior, I surrender all."

–Judson W. Van DeVenter

I love this song, but surrendering isn't always easy for me. The word surrender means to yield, to give up, to abandon.

Along with some dear friends, Chris and I were scheduled last fall to travel to Asia. We had been planning the details of the trip with them for a year and were excited about the ministry opportunities. Plane tickets were purchased, hotel reservations made, and the conferences we were hosting were in place. The previous May, Chris and I had applied for three-year visas in South Africa. Yet five months later, we were still waiting for our application to be completed. If we left South Africa without the visas, we would be branded as "undesirables" and not permitted to return for five years. We could not make the trip. Our friends traveled without us. The two of them did the work of four people. They spoke at numerous conferences and retreats and did a wonderful job. In fact, they took the ministry in that country to a whole new spiritual level.

In the midst of the confusion, I tried to surrender. The Bible tells us in Psalm 37:7 (GW): *"Surrender yourself to the LORD, and wait patiently for Him…"* The passage emphasizes staying focused on the LORD's goodness in your work and not being preoccupied with the difficulty at hand. I struggled because I was preoccupied and focused on getting to Asia. Instead of refocusing on the LORD, I focused all the more on the travel. I felt like I was surrendering every few minutes, yet my heart was filled with unrest and grief. I made phone calls, recruited South African friends to help, and visited the local Home Affairs office so many times that the officials knew me by name. I cried. I was so stressed that the people around me became stressed.

The last verse of "I Surrender All" is very moving. *"All to Jesus I surrender. Now I feel the sacred flame. Oh, the joy of full salvation! Glory, glory, to His name!"* I want to do better at living a life of surrender. The next time I'm faced with a crisis, I want to boldly declare that I feel the sacred presence of God and am content to walk in the joy of salvation.

week 52 reflections

1. When you gave your life to Christ, you surrendered to His ways. Think about that time in your life, and describe how you felt as you yielded your life to the Son of God.

2. Why do you think people in our society have a difficult time "surrendering"?

3. Consider the culture Jesus lived in. In what ways was life the same as today? In what ways were things different?

4. Psalm 37:7 (ESV) states: *"Be still before the LORD and wait patiently for him; fret not yourself over the one who prospers in his way, over the man who carries out evil devices!"* Do you find yourself "fretting" when you watch the nightly news and see the evil of men and their "evil devices"? What can you do to alleviate this stress and surrender all to God?

Tonya Jewel Blessing

National/International Speaker

Author of 1920's Appalachian Novel: The Whispering of the Willows
Co-Founder/Co-Director Strong Cross Ministries

Tonya grew up in rural Ohio. She currently lives in South Africa with her husband of 34 years. Tonya asked Jesus into her heart at the age of four. As a young adult, she worked for a well-known television evangelist, and traveled with a Christian drama group throughout the Midwest. Tonya has worked as a children's pastor, youth pastor, and women's pastor. She served on staff at Praise Church in Littleton, Colorado for a number of years. She also worked as the Director of Women's Ministries for Journey Church in Strasburg, Colorado, and has served on a number of ministry boards that support concerns for women. Tonya and her husband operated Strong Cross Ranch Colorado for over eleven years, a place of respite for missionaries and ministers. They had the honor of hosting over 2,000 guests during that time frame. The Blessings relocated their ministry to South Africa in June of 2012. The ministry continues to serve and partner with local pastors and missionaries. The Blessings oversee building projects, feeding programs, educational services, local churches, and a variety of other ministries. Tonya is a well-known national and international speaker, and is also a published author. She was ordained in 2011 and is currently pursuing further pastoral and biblical studies.

For additional information regarding Strong Cross Ministries South Africa, please visit the ministry web page – www.strongcrossministries.org. Tonya enjoys speaking and sharing her life with women at retreats and events. She thinks that women are amazing, and appreciates that the female gender is multifaceted yet fragile creations of God. In her personal life and as a speaker, Tonya believes that God's Word is powerful, and needs to be read and written on her heart and on the hearts of women everywhere. Contact Tonya through her website – www.tonyajewelblessing.com.

Sue Summers

Media Alert! 200 Activities to Create Media-savvy Kids
Changing the World through Media Education
Get Them Thinking! Use Media Literacy to Prepare Students for State Assessments

Sue Summers is a life-long educator. Sue has served for many years as graduate school instructor, Sunday school teacher, and elementary school library media specialist. She is Director of Media Alert! and the author of several books and many articles on media literacy (published under the name, Sue Lockwood Summers). Her passion is training adults who are in positions of influence (such as parents, grandparents, teachers, and youth pastors) to integrate media literacy – critical thinking about the messages of the media – into all subject areas and both formal and informal discussions. Sue served 17 years as Co-director of the non-profit, PRIIME TIIME Today, the Colorado media literacy outreach to students.

Sue is the recipient of the "Leaders in Learning Award" to honor her lifetime of leadership in media literacy education. This award was presented by the National Parent Teacher Association (PTA) and Cable in the Classroom in Washington, D.C.

Her outreach includes ladies' retreat leader, conference speaker, and church and PTA presenter. In addition, she is currently authoring a series of children's books that will challenge elementary-aged children to learn about living things and be glad they are who they are.

Sue lives in Littleton, Colorado, and enjoys volunteering, traveling, reading, and interacting with her four extraordinary grandchildren.

WE LIKE AMAZON.COM REVIEWS

GO TO:

FOR MORE GREAT BOOK SELECTIONS!

CPSIA information can be obtained
at www.ICGtesting.com
Printed in the USA
FFHW012214120919
54844112-60555FF

9 780997 897630